DENNIS E. GOLDEN JENNIFER J. LOWNIK

What To
Know
Do *And*
Say

To Be Safe

A Woman's Guide To Personal Safety

ISBN: 149923144X
ISBN 13: 9781499231441
Library of Congress Control Number: 2014907603
CreateSpace Independent Publishing Platform
North Charleston, South Carolina

Table of Contents

Forward

When it comes to women's personal safety, it has become fashionable to stress the need for self-defense training. While the suggestion appears to make sense, few of us have the time to become proficient enough to ward off a determined attacker using a combination of hit-and run techniques.

A well-known fact is that martial arts training bears little to no resemblance to real world encounters with muggers, batterers, or home invaders. I have known several women who, in spite of holding advanced martial arts degrees, found they were not emotionally prepared for a real encounter.

While the physical benefits of martial training are positive, the reality of the situation is that you are more likely to be stalked by a former partner, become a victim of workplace violence, or be victimized while traveling far more often than being assaulted by a stranger. If you are targeted, it most likely will be by someone you know. The good news is that sexual assaults committed by strangers are the easiest to avoid and yet it is the one most women fear.

Still another emerging trend is the growing number of women who are turning to firearms training for self-defense. While many firmly believe they could defend themselves, Lt. Col. Dave Grossman, the author of "On Killing," correctly points out that only 1% of the total population is capable of actually using deadly force when called upon. The willingness to deliberately take another's life or maim another human being when defending against a determined attacker is something that most women and men find repulsive.

Because armed or unarmed self-defenses are not always the best alternatives, this book fills an important niche by giving you access to one of the best self-defense tools the world has ever known—**the human mind and your ability to plan for and manage uncertainty and danger.** It is a tool you always have with you and, when properly trained, it will keep you trouble free 95% of the time.

While there can never be a 100% guarantee that the methods suggested here or elsewhere will be successful in every situation—being aware and prepared will put you at a distinct advantage over those who have never considered planning for the unexpected.

Women by nature have an incredible ability to see the hidden meaning behind words and pick up on subtle non-verbal clues such as body language and posture, tone of voice and more. The most important lesson women can take away from this remarkable book is to always listen to your built-in early warning system.

Introduction

It's called the Bronx and it's the northernmost of the five boroughs in the City of New York. Most people are surprised to learn that it is the third most densely populated county in the United States. At the same time, a quarter of the area is open green space and includes: Woodlawn Cemetery, Van Cortland Park, Reservoir Oval Park, Pelham Bay Park, the New York Botanical Garden, and the Bronx Zoo.

This entire area is connected by waking paths, bike trails, and paved streets. Growing up in this part of the city allowed me to spend hours on my bike, exploring the lakes, rivers and other sights and sounds found throughout the area. Back then no one gave much thought about personal safety. As long as I was home before the streetlights went on, it was presumed everything was okay.

While most of my adventures were uneventful, there were several occasions that gave me pause. Even in the late 50s, the isolated parks attracted some unsavory characters along with an interesting assortment of neighoood bullies who were always on the lookout for easy targets. Fortunately, a good three-speed bike usually put some distance between me and any potential danger. Little did I know that these early adventures would become a personal safety learning lab that would be used later in life.

My grandfather, Harry Golden, fit the profile of a 1920s New York City Irish Police Officer. At 6'4" and weighting 225 pounds, he was a commading figure. Like many in his time, he believed there was more justice at the end of a policeman's nightstick than could be found in all the law books in the City of New York. While those standards would cause more than a few raised eyebrows today, criminals of that era knew and understood how these interactions would end.

Harry lived and worked in a section of the city known as Hell's Kitchen. The mostly Irish community was notorious for assaulting unwelcome guests and police officers by raining down a storm of bricks from tenement rooftops. At the same time, one of the best ways for youths to escape the economic and social pressures of "The Kitchen" was to pursue a career in law enforcement or join the New York City Fire Department.

My father, Gene Golden, and his two brothers, Harry and Larry, were no exception. While today's inner city youths pursue basketball as a way out of poverty, Harry, Larry, and Gene spent most of their free time studying and working out in preparation for the physical portion of the New York City police and fire examinations.

While Dad passed both the police and fire physicals, he decided that public service was not his calling and eventually took a job with a Wall Street bank. Given his family background and physical size, it wasn't long before he settled into corporate security. It proved to be a good match and within a few years, he led a worldwide corporate security division.

In the 1960s, the family moved to Pelham, New York, a small bucolic community in southern Westchester County, a stones throw from New York City. Our weekly family gatherings often included my grandparents. To say these family get-togethers were interesting would be an understatement. Just think of the CBS show "Blue Bloods" and you have a picture of a Sunday afternoon dinner at the Golden's.

One Sunday curiosity got the best of me and I casually asked what type of crimes could possibly occur inside a Wall Street Bank. Much to my surprise the answer was "every type of crime that happens on the street can and does happen inside those walls." In a single year, my father had investigated assaults, rapes, drug use, petty thefts, armed robberies, black mail, and extortion not to mention holdups and the theft of millions of dollars in securities. "The only crimes that don't happen inside of our buildings are auto accidents." After a long pause, he added, "That's because the employees can't get their cars through the front doors." Okay, another lesson learned. **Criminals are found everywhere and appearances can be deceiving. Crooks, just like ice cream, come in all flavors and can be well dressed and well educated**.

Due to dad's interactions with various law enforcement agencies, our home was often a gathering place where weekend visitors included FBI agents, postal inspectors, prison wardens, chiefs of police, sheriffs, secret service agents, judges, district attorneys, and more.

It was always fascinating to listen to the various stories law enforcement officers told. Some were funny, others eye-opening and still others were unbelieveable. The details of each account left an impression and without my knowing it, these stories were forming the foundation of what I would later call an *Experience Library*.

After completing graduate school, I pursued a career in Marketing and Sales. Any thoughts or concerns for my personal safety no longer appeared to be important. I was married, lived in a safe neighborhood, had a great career, and never dealt with criminal types. Little thought was given to my long forgotten *Experiences.*

All that changed on a cold November day in New York City when I found myself becoming ill. Knowing I had a long commute back to Connecticut, I canceled my afternoon appointments and proceeded to the nearest subway station. It did not take long for a subway to arrive to take me to Grand Central Station. Just as the car doors closed, a young man stepped in and sat directly across from me. Given the entire car was empty, I found his behavior to be somewhat strange. Throughout the ride, he continually checked his watch and would look at me and smile. Minutes before we were to arrive at Grand Cental Station, he bolted from his seat, pointed a knife at me and demanded money.

All at once, I was overwhelmed with a mix of emotions ranging from fear to anger. The last thing I wanted to do was deal with him. It was at that moment I remembered my grandfather saying, "All criminals have three fears. Always take advantage of that weakness." What most people don't understand is that criminals have a well-thought-out game plan and, for the most part, know how a potential victim will react when threatened. If you, as a potential target, begin acting out of character, a number of warning flares go up and criminals will often back off.

To this day I don't know how the exact words came to mind. I was too sick to show fear. As I spoke, the expression on his face changed as he realized something was going wrong with his plan. Within seconds he sensed that he had moved from the position of predator to becoming prey. Looking at me in disbelief he steped back and put the knife back in his pocket. He said, "So sorry. I was just kidding—just having some fun." He apologized a second time and bolted off the subway car as the doors opened.

So what did I say? What did I do? Why did that predator suddenly walk away? The answer to those questions and more will be found later in this book.

Hopefully you will find this volume to be a useful guide on how by simply changing your view of the world, you can successfully impact the outcome of many potentially dangerous situations—at work, at play and in life.

Let us begin our journey by examing a well-established myth that politicians and media folks like to tell us. **"There is no need to worry—we have police deparments who are there to protect you."**

"Police officers have NO duty to protect the citizens of this country."

United States Supreme Court

1

Personal Safety – Your Responsibility

Jared Diamond in his book, "The World Until Yesterday", points out that people who live in primitive societies develop what he calls a "positive form of constructive paranoia" at a very young age. Loosely defined, it means, if you want to survive, you must learn how to avoid the cumulative effects of engaging in any type of precarious behavior, no matter how trivial it might appear at the time.

Diamond illustrates this life lesson by pointing out that individuals who live in the jungle know that high humidity, rainfall, and heat cause otherwise large, healthy looking trees to suddenly fall over without warning. If you spend most of your life gathering food in a tropical rainforest, and you want to live another day, you learn not to camp or seek shelter from the blazing sun under large shade trees.

In contrast, we live in a sanitized technological society and presume that there is no need for us to practice constructive paranoia. We are more prone to routinely take small risks and have learned that we can walk away with no apparent consequences. What we tend to overlook is the fact that over time, repeating risky behavior will catch up with us.

Living in Western civilization presents its own unique set of challenges that are as dangerous as falling trees. Unfortunately, our lifestyle makes it easy for us to miss the many subtle warning signs that danger is present. Yet, by simply being more observant, it would be relatively easy for women to significantly reduce many risks to their personal safety and security. The good news is that you do not have to go into a doomsday prepper mode to accomplish this. All one needs to do is be willing to make small changes in your daily patterns.

Our Western culture affords us an opportunity to engage in a lifestyle that is rather comfortable and convenient. It is easy for us to choose the path of least resistance. We may, for example, choose to eat convenience foods verses a heathier alternative. We may prefer to jump into our car verses choosing the more healthy alternative of walking a few blocks to a nearby location. Every day our modern lives are surrounded by a host of distractions that draw our attention away from the need to be safe. In short, most of us routinely ignore life's warning signs as we set up camp and seek shelter under the big trees of modern society.

Like it or not, we live in a world that is becoming increasing hostle to women's personal safety and security. According to the Rape Abuse & Incest Network (RAINN), the nation's largest anti-sexual violence organization, one out of every six women has been the victim of an attempted rape. It does not stop there. Danger can visit us in many ways.

Reflect for moment as to the number of times you simply slowed down for a stop sign rather than coming to a complete stop. Consider the number of times you neglected to buckle your seatbelt for a short trip and disregarded the fact that most fatal accidents happen within a mile from home. Who has not answered a cell phone, did a make-up check in the rearview mirror, or looked at a quick text message while driving? While these actions are dangerous, we comfort ourselves knowing that bad things always happen to "the other guy."

At the core of our thinking lies a faulty assumption that in times of danger, emergency help is always nearby. We carry our personal cell phones and iPads in our purses and trust that we can summon help at a moment's notice. If seriously injured, we might find ourselves being taken by a LifeStar helicopter to a state-of-the-art medical center where teams of emergency medical providers will battle to save our lives. While access to technology medical care is comforting, our ability to communicate anywhere in the world has served to blunt our need to be more aware of the world around us.

Most crimes occur in a matter of seconds. At the same time, police response is often measured in minutes, hours, or not at all, depending on distance and the competence of the 911 operator. Women often presume the police are there to protect us but are unaware of the fact that for the past 30 years the U.S. Supreme Court has consistently ruled that your local police department has no legal obligation to protect private citizens.

If you are the victim of a sexual assault, for example, you can not file a lawsuite against your local police department for failing to protect you or your family. Legally, the only job the police can be held responsible for is their obligations to act prudently, investigate crimes, and arrest those who break the law. The only time police must protect you is if they take you into custody or prevent you from driving if they discover you are intoxicated or under the influence of drugs. Most folks are taken aback when they learn the simple truth. **We are all on our own when it comes to personal safety.**

So where do you begin your journey?

The fact that you are reading this book says you are on the right path. Chances are good you depend on yourself and have recognized that others depend on you. It might be your elderly parents, children, friends, or siblings who rely on you for support. It is also highly likely you embrace a lifestyle that supports the belief that being aware and prepared is a personal RESPONSIBILITY. In all likelyhood you view making a committment to individual safety in much the same way as you might make a committment to take care of your health by being physically active, eating properly, and getting regular medical checkups.

Consider incorporating one or more of the following into your daily or weekly routine. Each application is designed to further sharpen your awarness skills.

- Keep and periodically read a daily journal that documents both your concerns and your observations regarding personal safety.
- Begin traveling alone to new locations where you will have opportunities to ask yourself, "What would I do if I only had myself to depend on?"
- Attempt new experiences that will challenge you to reach beyond your routine comfort zone.
- Seek out others who both share and disagree with your personal safety concerns. Doing so will force you to reconsider where you stand on various issues.

As you start to engage in life differently, you will begin to put yourself in the forefront when it comes to personal security. Remember, no matter your age or physical condition, you can begin to take small steps today that will allow you to develop a mindset that will help you survive in a world that is becoming increasingly more hostile to you and your family.

CHAPTER EXERCISE

✓ *What five things can you do this week to change your daily routines?*

✓ *How can a personal journal make you more aware?*

✓ *Write down at least 10 risky things you have done in the past 30 days.*

✓ *How can traveling alone help women become more aware of the need for personal safety?*

✓ *Who is responsible for your personal safety?*

"Everything you can imagine is real."

Pablo Picasso

2

Building An "Experience Library"

If you have been to a public library, you know that the information and books are arranged by author and subject. You will find children's books in one section, reference books in another, and books on decorating and fashion in another. The library uses this system to make it easy for visitors to find what they are looking for.

An "Experience Library," often called the library of the mind, does not store information on neat shelves. An "Experience Library" does not separate fact from fiction. All information is stored in one large file called life experiences. When a situation arises, our brain automatically begins a search to discover how we reacted to the same or similar experience in the past. Given normal circumstances, we will come up with a solution or method in a matter of seconds. The trouble begins when our mental search encounters an empty file and there is nothing to draw upon. Finding an empty file causes us to pause as our brain begins to assemble disparate experiences in an effort to formulate a new solution. Those few seconds of delay, as you will see later, can sometimes mean the difference between surviving or not.

Here is how the "Experience Library" gets its information:

- A **direct experience** is one in which you have personally interacted with people, places, or things around you. If you were a girl who lived in a cave during prehistoric times, you learned at a young age that touching the red and orange flames was an experience you did not want to repeat. You learned first hand to respect fire and all things that are hot.
- An **indirect experience** is one where you learn as a result of another's interaction with people, places, or things. For fun, let's go back to our cave and pretend we are listening to a member of the clan telling the story of a young girl from another village who picked up a baby bear. We learn from the storyteller that the mama grizzly decided that she needed to end the interaction the only way she knew how. The graphic details of this encounter would be shared as an indirect experience in the hope that no one from your village would suffer the same fate.

Our ability as humans to learn lessons directly and indirectly allows us to play out different scenarios in our minds and to think about how we might react in different or similar situations. The more detailed we are in visualizing how we might react to a future event, the more deeply embedded the experience is etched in our library.

The key to this type of learning is to think through and visualize as much detail as possible when you are formulating a response or solution. Once an initial solution has been reached, you will want to come up with a second or third solution to the same problem. Having a range of options in your "Experience

Library" can prove to be a lifesaver as it will allow you to come up with a variety of creative solutions in a matter of sconds. Here is how one experience library saved over 2,000 lives.

On September 11, 2001 at 8:46 in the morning, American Airlines flight 11 struck Tower 1 of the World Trade Center. Rick Rescorla, Vice President for Security at Morgan Stanley, Dean Witter heard the explosion and saw the north tower burning from his office windows. When the announcement came over the public address system urging people to stay at their desks in Tower 2, Rescorla ignored the announcement, grabbed his bullhorn, walkie-talkie and cell phone, and began systematically ordering Morgan Stanley employees to evacuate, including 1,000 employees in 5 World Trade Center. He directed people down a stairwell from the 44th floor, and continued to calm employees as the building lurched violently following the crash of a second plane 38 floors above them.

Morgan Stanley Executive Vice President Bill McMahon stated that even a group of 250 people who were visiting for a stock-broker training class knew what to do because they had been shown the nearest stairway.

After successfully evacuating 2,687 employees, Rescorla went back into the building to make sure that everyone else was out. He was last seen on the 10th floor heading up, shortly before the tower collapsed. His remains were never recovered. Rick was declared dead three weeks following the attacks.

The actions of Rick Rescorla are dramatic examples of the benefit of having a plan in place before you need one. While Morgan Stanley employees often chided Rick for his insistance on repeated company-wide drills, the fact that he made everyone participate demonstates the value of having a safety plan. Rick never knew what he was planning for, but his preparation saved thousands of lives.

A similar story can be told about Kate, a young woman who attended one of our women's travel safety workshops. She was going to visit Haiti and was concerned about her personal safety due to the potential for earthquakes. We laid out several approaches and suggested that she develop an action plan before she needed one.

On the day of her arrival in Haiti, she was checking into a local hotel when she felt the first tremor. Without giving it a second thought Kate removed her high-heel shoes, turned, and ran out of the building and stood in the street. Her pre-plan was a simple one. "Where ever I am, I will try to run outside at the first tremor." Her traveling companions and other hotel guests who were standing in the lobby looked at her in disbelief. Within minutes, the entire building collapsed taking the lives of those who remained in the building.

In addition to having a plan, Kate took it further and created what we call a "reaction trigger." Simply defined, a reaction trigger is the thing that will make you react without giving it a second thought. To understand this concept, imagine you are driving and the car in front of you suddenly stops. Without thinking, you would automatically step on your break to avoid a collision. This built-in reaction trigger is so strong and automatic that you will react the same way by stepping on an imaginary break even when sitting in the passenger seat.

Cade Cortley in his book "Seal Survival Guide" discusses how Navy SEALs use something called emergency conditioning [EC] to prepare themselves for survival situations. Basically, EC is a way to condition your mind in advance to be prepared with a course of action to meet any emergency you think you may face. Having one or more plans in place immediately produces a profound psychological strength and experience base that can be drawn upon without thinking. Any plan you develop in advance may not be an exact remedy for a particular situation; however, the fact that you have a rudimentary plan of action in place, puts you miles ahead when you need it most.

Countless studies have been done on why some people survive a dangerous situation while others do not. All research points to the fact that those who had planned ahead were the ones who survived. Often the slightest hesitation can result in the loss of life.

The following is another example of why you may want to have a safety plan in place before you need one.

What kills the vast majority of passengers in a plane crash is not the actual impact. Fatalities are often the direct result of the fire that eventually engulfs the plane. Having survived the initial impact, most people relax and mistakenly believe they are safe while underestimating how quickly a fire can spread. FAA surveys show that most people think they have about thirty minutes to get out of a burning plane. The reality is that it takes less than two minutes for a fire to burn through the plane's fuselage. Having that type of information in advance along with having a plan in place could save your life some day.

CHAPTER EXERCISE

✓ What items of clothing and footwear might hinder a woman from quickly exiting a plane in the case of an emergency?

✓ How would you react if you suddenly faced an armed attacker?

✓ How would you find a lost family member following a disaster?

✓ Where would you find water if your normal source was suddenly gone?

✓ What would you do if, due to a disaster, you lost electric power for several weeks?

"I rely far more on gut instinct than researching huge amounts of statistics."

Sir Richard Branson

3

Being Aware – It's More Than You Think

Let's start with the basics. The military defines situational awareness as the ability to identify, process, and comprehend critical elements of information about what is happening around you. That is a good start. The vast majority of people choose to live in an insulated world and are totally oblivious to what is happening around them. Most of us have seen people glued to their cell phones while walking, jogging, or riding a bike. Many of us were amused to see a woman featured on the news who was so engrossed in texting while walking in a shoping mall, she fell into a reflecting pool. Who among us has not seen a driver reading maps or newspapers or applying makeup while speeding along the highway at upwards of 60 miles per hour? Does it really come as a shock when we learn that unattentive people are often the ones victimized by crime?

Every place you travel or visit demands a different level of awareness. While you are sitting at home you should be able to enjoy the safety and security that environment offers. At the same time, do not make the mistake of allowing yourself to think that all "safe" places are secure. Women have a naturally occuring built in-radar system that is extremely effective for detecting danger and avoiding perilous situations. You can increase sensitivity to your surroundings by practicing a few simple drills.

Situational awareness is a learned physical skill that can be self-taught. A simple approach begins with carrying a 3 x 5 index card in your purse at all times. Each time you are caught unaware, write down the date and time. Every time someone approaches you without your first noticing them, write down the date and time. While driving to work, try randomly asking yourself exactly where you are on a highway at that given moment and could you give someone specific directions on how to find you? Can you recall what exit you just passed or could you tell someone the mile marker on the road? After 30 days, look at your card(s). You will discover that your surprise events are becoming noticeably less frequent. After 60 days you will be amazed at your increased levels of awareness of people and events in your world.

Another way to improve your situational awareness level is to observe others and think about how you and they might react. If you were in a shopping center with some of your girlfriends, ask yourself where would you go to take immediate cover. As you look around ask yourself why someone might be behaving in a particular manner. You might see someone wearing a long coat and ask why would someone dress that way on such a hot day. Try to guess what people might be thinking and make an effort to anticipate their next move. The more you practice situational awareness and share your observations with others, the more you will hone skills that will far exceed what most people posses in a lifetime.

Improving situational awareness skills is just the first step. Your next task is to learn how to trust your women's intuition and listen to that small voice inside of you that says, "Be careful—do something different."

Personal security experts who deal with terrorism, report that people can generally sense potentially dangerous situations and individuals long before something actually happens. Prior to the attacks on the World Trade Center in New York City, scientsts and engineers working on the Global Consciouness Project knew something significant was about to happen somewhere in the world. For those of you not familiar with The Global Consciousness Project, it is an international, multi-disciplinary collaboration of scientists and engineers who collect numerical data from a global network of 70 host sites. The second-by-second data is transmitted to a central archive where researchers can see if a significant event is about to take place. The resulting evidence from this research suggests that there is a worldwide unifying awareness of impending potential danger that reaches across all nations and cultures.

On a more practical level let us imagine that your daughter has worked late one evening and must take an elevator to get to her car. When the doors open, she sees a man inside and her immediate reaction is fear. More often than not, most women will say to themselves, "Oh, I'm just being silly and letting my imagination get the best of me." She then proceeds to close herself up in a metal box with a stranger and discovers moments later that the voice in her head was accurate.

We all possess the gift of intuition and can detect signals long before our logical minds have the time to process what is really going on. While we cannot logically describe what makes up these feelings of discomfort, all women would be wise to **avoid the following traps:**

▓ **Not Listening To That Small Voice.** Becoming sensitive to your intuition or gut feelings is all about a willingness to listen to yourself. Sometimes you may get a "don't go there" or "something's fishy about this" message. These are called caution signals. Sometimes, like Sir Richard Branson, billionaire founder of The Virgin Group, a conglomerate of over 400 companies, the small voice inside his head says, "This is a great idea. Let's explore it." When asked how they came up with a successful idea or invention, many successful entrepreneurs and business people will often say they just had a hunch they might be successful. Some people believe intuition is a spiritual voice. Others call it an inner voice or sixth sense. Either way, you are well advised to listen to it.

▓ **Not Exercising Your Intuitive Skills**. Think of intuition as an inner muscle. If you don't use it, it becomes weak and harder to hear. Respect your intuition, act on it, and do not pay attention to what others may say or think. Start with simple things. For example, if your intuition says, "Don't take the freeway today," take an alternate route. Some days you will be surprised to find out there was an accident on the freeway. Other days, nothing may have apparently happened and that is okay. What's important is that you are slowly strengthening your intuition. Over time, you are more apt to hear valuable messages and information that could safe your life.

CHAPTER EXERCISE

✓ How often have you regretted not following your woman's intuition?

✓ Do you think it is silly to listen to your feelings?

✓ How has listening to your inner voice helped you? Be specific.

✓ What is holding you back from sharing your thoughts with others?

"The key to change ... is to let go of fear."

Rosanne Cash

4

Embracing Fear

Fear is a word people use rather loosely. Most of the time what they are talking about is anxiety about a future event, or they may be recalling a negative feeling from the past. In contrast, true fear is a warning sign intended to cause either an action or reaction such as fight or run. Unfortunately, many women choose to live their life in a constant state of fear. When something truly dangerous comes along, they discover that there are no new signals to provide an additional level warning when needed.

There are real differences between caution and fear.

- Caution is more of a general alarm that keeps you in tune with your surroundings. You are aware of what is happening around you but you are not jumping to conclusions.
- Fear, on the other hand, is very different and can often lead to panic thinking. Reacting to fear can actually be more dangerous than what you fear. Consider for a moment what might happen if you stood near the edge of cliff and cautiously looked over the edge. While you might feel some initial distress, you know

that your use of caution has you in compete control of the situation.

For a number of years I was an adjunct instructor at several universities where I taught public speaking and group communications. Each semester there was always a group of female students who left taking the manditory public speaking class for the last semester, even though they could have taken it early in their sophmore year. I often asked myself why did these intelligent women have such a profound fear of speaking. Over time it became clear to me that these women were not afraid of public speaking. The real fear centered on the possibility that they would perform badly in front of their classmates. In short, they believed that would be seen as "not being good enough."

The fear of speaking is really more than just embarrassment. It is all about the fear of being perceived as someone who is incompetent. When a student would say they were afraid of speaking, a few well-placed questions usually helped them get over their initial hesitation. The first question was, "Would you be terrified if you found yourself trapped in a building during an earthquake with no way out?" Almost all said yes. The next question was, "Are you afraid an earthquake might hit right now?" The answer was always no. By drawing such a comparison, the students began to realize that a fear of something that might happen was quite different than something that was about to happen. Once they understood that everyone has some apprehension about public speaking, they realized they could easily overcome fear simply by aquiring knowledge about their topic.

The next time you use the word fear, stop and ask yourself if you are manufacturing that fear or is there something you really need to be fearful about. The only time fear should be accepted as a valid emotion is when you perceive that your life or personal safety of someone close to you is in immediate danger.

When you begin to understand how fear can help you avoid real dangers, you put yourself in a better position. With your mind free of manufactured distractions, you are better able to think clearly and creatively about how you might approach a challenge or handle an unexpected event.

Having spent a number of years training and preparing for the worst possible events, I have come to the conclusion that while the world is a dangerous place, it can be safe—if you are willing to pay attention to what is happening around you.

Consider the fact we routinely drive cars on high-speed high-ways. We ride in commercial planes that travel miles above the earth. We ride elevators and trust that the cables will hold us up. Stop and think about how we put our lives at risk with any number of sports. Every day we are surrounded by toxic chemicals. Our homes are heated by furnaces and hot water heaters that could explode at a moment's notice. The key to living in a world that is becoming increasingly more danger-ous is to recognize that women's intuition is an excellent guide to both recognizing danger and controlling our fear. Listen to your inner voice and learn to act without second-guessing your decisions.

Conquering Fear

Animals, unlike humans, only exhibit fear when they are facing immediate danger. We, on the other hand, are the only species who can fear something that *might* happen at some time in the future. Some anthropologists say this type of apprehension is necessary as it can prevent us from doing something we might regret. When you really stop and think about it, the vast majority of fears is baseless and holds us back.

When people are asked what they fear, their responses will include: speaking in public, fear of failure, rejection, death, intimacy, success, loss of income, and being seen as not good enough.

If you lay all fears and concerns aside, the last thing on the list, "not being seen as good enough," is the foundation upon which all others are based. That single roadblock can stop you every time. It is important to understand that you are not alone in harboring these feelings. Some of the most successful people, including J.K. Rowling, the author of the "Harry Potter" series of seven books, noted that she lived with fear every day, although she did not show it. Once you understand that the fear of being seen as not good enough is what holds you back.

Here are some suggestions on how you can begin managing your fears.

- **Embrace them**. Acknowledge and recognize that you're not alone and that we ALL have fears. Understand that fear is part of being human. Once recognized for what it is, you can begin to move forward by not letting it control you.
- **Acknowledge them.** Fear is an enemy that has a way of establishing an outpost in our heads, where it lives unacknowledged. By moving our fears out into the light of day, by writing them down, you will begin to

recognize them for what they are. Some people will take their fear sheets and burn them as a symbolic way to say, "I have now conquered those fears."

- **Ask yourself:** What's the **worst** thing that can happen? As soon as you take the time to calmly evaluate the many outcomes that are available, you will discover it is never as bad as originally thought.
- **Prepare yourself.** If you were going to run a race, you would take the time to be prepared. You would train, practice, and come up with a plan to succeed. When you are looking at the challenge of conquering fear, the same level of preparation will help you to succeed.
- **Build your experience library**. Stop worrying about what *might* happen. Focus on how you will respond to the particular challenge. Write it down, make adjustments, and come up with several options. After you write them down, recognize that you have done all you can do. Place them in your experience library. Put concerns aside. It is time to move on.
- **Take small steps**. Start small. Do something you know you can succeed at. Enjoy the moment and take another small step. Keep doing this, and soon you will have chipped away at what holds you back.

CHAPTER EXERCISE

✓ What is the difference between fear and anxiety?

✓ Name three ways to conquer fear.

✓ Why would you embrace fear in your life?

✓ Are you holding yourself back over a concern of not being good enough?

✓ Write down three fears that are holding you back and ask yourself why?

"It's Not WHAT You Said It's HOW You Said It."

Anonymous

5

It's Not What You Said

By now, you probably have lost count of the number of times you have been offended or hurt by something someone has said to you. Chances are good that you might have been wrongly accused or perhaps you might have been on the receivng end of someone else's bad day.

Typical responses to these and other verbal attacks might be:

- Remain silent until the tirade is over and go about your business.
- Come back full force with a similar statement, presented in a similar tone and fashion.

Unfortunately, neither of the above approaches solves the problem nor will they allow you to take control of the situation or discover what might be the root cause of the issue at hand.

- By not responding, you send a silent signal that it is acceptable for someone to continue their verbal abuse. If an agressor believes he or she has the upper hand, the verbal attack will often escalate. This type of verbal tactic is a clasic technique and is most often used by bullies and abusers who are attempting to exert control over a victim.

▪ Responding back in kind and meeting force with force will immediately escalate the situation. At this point, neither party is taking the time to listen to what the other has to say. The "I can yell louder then you approach" quickly polarizes both parties, creates enemies, and leads to the risk of physical violence.

So if neither response is appropriate, what is the best way to respond to any aggressive verbal encounter? The answer may surprise you.

Let us begin with the observation that our lives are shaped by our personal experiences, backgrounds, training, language, culture, values, upbringing, education, and more. As a result of these influences, we see and react to things in ways that are unique to us. So profound are these personal experiences that children growing up in the same home, with the same parents, will display dissimilar personality traits. How many parents do you know have commented that each of their children see life differently?

A simple demonstration on how experiences vary can be illustrated using a playing card. Begin by showing somone the back of the card. Then ask them to describe what they see. Repeat the exercise, showing them a new card. They will say it looks the same. Each card will look different from your perspective than from the other person's perspective. Even though you are both looking at the same card, each is having a different visual experience. If you translate this simple exercise into life experiences, you can begin to see why each of us will describe identical experiences differently.

When people are distraught and engaged in a heated conversation, there is a natural tendency for all parties to focus on the words being said. During a heated conversation, with your husband, for example, you mght find yourself firing back replies or making statements without stopping to ask yourself, "What is behind the anger or frustration that he is expressing?"

To successfully engage in a conversation, you must be prepared to listen, not just hear sounds. By definition, hearing is an involuntary natural act, over which we have no control. If we have normal hearing, our ears will, through no effort on our part, detect sounds. Listening, on the other hand, requires focus and demands that we make a concentrated effort to pay close attention to what is being communicated. When people are asked the question, "What is the opposite of speaking?" most proudly say listening. While that response is correct, it rarely describes what people are actually doing.

Studies show that when we are engaged in any conversation, 95% of us are not listening. Instead of paying attention and providing meaningful feedback, we are waiting for a break in the noise so we can insert our opinion. We also fail to recognize that we are not alone in this exchange because the other person to whom we are speaking is doing the same thing. Rather than recognizing what the real issues are, we tell ourselves the other person is just being difficult.

In case you have not noticed, we all deal with difficult people every day. We meet them at work, at home, in school, while we are out shopping, and when we travel. Yet, in spite of our overwhelming need to properly connect with others, few of us ever have an opportunity in our academic experience to take a class on how to properly communicate or respond to other people.

Without some type of formal instruction, we experiment with different approaches and, for better or worse, we develop our own highly personal approach. If you are like most people, the chances are that your reactions and responses are doing more harm than good. To put it another way, *if you feel you are winning arguments by putting others in their place, you are losing the arguments and potentially creating enemies.*

President Richard Nixon once declared, "I'm not a crook" when he was asked about the Watergate break-ins. Instead of telling the truth during the initial phase of the investigation, he found himself caught in a no-win scenario and a never-ending politically charged environment. In the long run it was his **words,** not his actions, that caused his downfall. Bill Clinton and his famous verbal joust with Congress on the meaning of the word "IS" provides a more recent example on how words can impact careers. It did not take long after his verbal jousting that his license to practice law was suspended. It is important to remember that your words have meaning. What you say and how you say it can impact you and others for a lifetime.

Before we can discuss **how** it might be best to interact with people, let us begin by identifying three different types:

- **Nice people** are reasonable and logical. For the most part they will do what you ask first time around. Nice people are gracious. They don't complain. Typically they have been successful in life because they developed an easy style when interacting with others.

Approximately 40% of the population fall into this category.

- **Difficult people** appear to be problematic and challenging. Their typical response to most requests is "Why?" Initially the question might appear to be a challenge but in reality what they are asking is, " What's in it for me." Rather than being perceived as a challenge, a better way to react is to look at their response as an opportunity to explain how they can benefit by listening to what you have to say. By approaching difficult people from the perspective of their need to know more, you can gain their cooperation and support. Approximately 50% of the population falls under this category.
- **Mischief-makers.** These are the most difficult people to deal with because your initial reaction is to overlook their actions. These are the folks who are always nice when meeting you face to face, but will complain about you to anyone who will listen. They will snip at you from a distance and try to undermine your position. Individuals who make up this group are always disruptive to any organization. Immediately ask them to clarify their position.

Whenever you deal with difficult people, you must force yourself to remain silent and train yourself to listen to what they are saying. As you listen, focus on their face and nod to indicate that you listening. Women have a significant advantage using this technique as they naturally are better listeners than men. Your nod does not signal agreement, rather you are providing physical confirmation that indicates to the other person you are both focused and listening. Forcing yourself to remain silent in the face of adversity is a learned physical skill that must be practiced. Over time, you will discover that this practiced skill will become a physical trigger that will serve to remind you to act differently as you interact with others.

Going silent and nodding also has the secondary advantage of giving you time to gain control of your emotions and turn off your hot buttons. Once you know you are under control, begin asking yourself additional questions such as, "Why is this person behaving this way?" or "How would I feel if I were in his or her position?" As you ask yourself these questions, you will begin to see things from a different perspective. Rather than viewing the individual as an opponent, you will begin to use one of the most poweful verbal defense tools—the ability to empathize with people by identifying and understanding another's situation, feelings, and motive. The ability to use empathy is extremely well suited to women due to their natural instinct to nurture.

To express empathy for an individual does not imply that you are being sympathetic to their cause or position. It does not suggest that you support their point of view. Displaying empathy at this juncture only suggests that you are trying to understand where an individual is coming from and that you are truly listening to the meaning of their words.

Key points to ponder:

- Empathy absorbs tension.
- Once an individual recognizes that you are genuinely interested in hearing what he has to say his general reaction is to calm down and become more reasonable.

- When expressing empathy <u>never use phrases</u> like "I understand" because the chances are you don't understand the background pressures that caused the outburst.

- Use phrases such as "I hear what you're saying" or "I see your point."

- The key with this approach is to remain absolutely neutral and not let pre-conceived ideas or opinions interfere with the communication.

CHAPTER EXERCISE

✓ What are your hot buttons?

✓ Why does going silent help you gain control?

✓ Why do you never say "I understand" if someone is agitated?

✓ Why is empathy such a powerfull tool for women?

"Whatever you wish that others would do to you, do also to them, for this is the Law and the Prophets."

Mathew 7:12

6

The Art of Dealing With Difficult People

After earning a Master's Degree in Communications from New York University, I was fairly confident in my ability to persuade and interact with people. Following my college experience, I went on to teach pubic speaking and group communications at several colleges and universities. One day, it hit me. All of the so-called tried and true effective communication styles that were being used bore little to no resemblance to real world communication. Practitioners of the martial arts often will make a similar observation. After spending years training, they suddenly come face to face with the reality that a real encounter with a street predator is quite different from the highly orchestrated and predictable scenarios practiced in training studios called dojos.

We only need to look at our political leaders to see how often these so-called trained professionals say things that should never have been said. We frequently hear someone from media relations come back to the press with a spin statement that says, "What Mr. X really meant to say was."

Even though I was a trained communications professional, I would often find myself in situations where my communication style was less than effective, particularly when interacting with people who did not share my point of view.

When encountering resistance, we routinely blurt out the first words that come to mind. Not long after, we typically regret what we said and how we said it. Words said in haste or in the heat of the moment can be cruel, cutting, and cause long-term damage to relationships. The reason these outbursts occur is that we allow others to set the tone during a conversation. We react and overlook a simple rule; *you cannot control a situation when you are out of control.*

Before you find yourself in the next heated verbal exchange, take some time and sit down with pen and paper and honestly identify your hot buttons. Ask yourself what statements or events trigger your responses during a heated conversation. Once you fully understand what phrases, actions, or tone of voice result in your loss of control, you will be able to incorporate some highly effective physical stop signs that will help remind you to get your temper and tongue under control.

As a first step, you will want to develop a physical posture that is not threatening and, at the same time, puts the other person at ease. Second, force yourself to go silent even if you find you are the target of insults or know what is being said is unfair or incorrect. Third, and this is difficult for women to do, ignore both the actual words and how those words are being said. Fourth, put your own prejudices, opinions, and preconceived ideas aside; you want to do everything in your power to physically and psychologically put yourself in neutral as the other is speaking. This step-by-step process takes practice but in the long run it will allow you to gain a better understanding of what is happening and you will have conquered your initial tendency to react or to speak negatively.

The Power of Paraphrasing

In most heated conversation there comes a time when due to frustration or anger, individuals will begin to repeat the same arguments and statements over and over again, Rather than allowing the conversation to disintegrate into a never-ending meaningless rehash, you can begin to take control by politely interrupting and playing back what was just said. You statements might sound something like this:

- "Excuse me ... Let me make sure I understand what you are saying."
- "Let me repeat that back to you."
- "Stop. Did you really mean to say that?"
- "I am not sure I understand. Is this what you mean?"

Whenever you paraphrase what someone else has said, it is important that you do not play back the exact same words. Repeating the identical phrases and words in the exact sequence can often be interpreted as a form of mockery. As a result, you can increase the level of discomfort and raise additional obstacles to an ongoing communication flow. Ideally you will want to present his argument differently and in your own words. Because women have a natural ability to understand the deeper meaning of words, they can use it to their advantage by making someone become part of a potential solution. If someone says, "I don't like the way you treat employees," you might play that back by saying, "I see you are concerned about employee treatment. Can you help me by offering some examples?"

Being proactive rather than reactive offers multiple benefits, some of which are listed below.

First. By demonstrating that you have been listening, you can now take control of the exchange. Because you are repeating the meaning of what was said versus parroting his exact words, the individual will focus on what you are saying to be sure that you properly understood the message.

Second. If you have misinterpreted what was said, the other individual now has an opportunity to correct any misunderstanding. By engaging in a back and forth dialogue, both parties are contributing to the exchange, providing both with a better opportunity to respond and clarify.

Third. You now have the other person's attention and by continuing to lower the tone of your voice, you will gradually be able to calm down any heated verbal exchange. At this point, you might suggest that you both go to a secondary location. Even if this distance is only a few feet away, it is a physical way to signal that progress is being made.

Fourth. Throughout this process you have moved the other individual from a speaker to a listener. At the same time you have created an atmosphere where empathy has taken the place of volatility. When successfully executed, the other person will begin to understand that you are trying to offer help as you are trying to comprehend his or her point of view.

Fifth. Paraphrasing has an unusual effect and quickly generates a sense of "fair play," as people will often respond in kind to each other. The approach can also result in them apologizing for their initial actions or indicating that their words and tone were inappropriate. Skilled paraphrasing alone can often de-escalate many encounters.

If you find that you are not making progress with someone, do not become frustrated. Go silent. State that you want some time to think over what has been said and leave the area.

CHAPTER EXERCISE

✓ *Why is conflict resolution an important skill for women?*

✓ *Why do we blurt out comments rather than listening?*

✓ *How can you control your hot buttons?*

✓ *How can you use the techniques in this chapter with your children or spouse?*

✓ *Why is going silent such a powerful tool for women?*

✓ *Why is paraphrasing such a powerful tool for women?*

"Survival is not about being fearless. It's about making a decision, getting on and doing it, because I want to see my kids again, or whatever the reason might be."

Bear Grylls

7

What It Means To Be Prepared

The two most frequently asked questions that come up during our workshops and programs are "What are some practical every day self-defense suggestions that women can use to protect themselves?" and "How can I protect my family when it comes to unexpected events?"

Best Self-Defense Tool

Anytime you are facing danger, whether it is natural or man made, your most prized weapon will not be a physical tool, a firearm, or a doomsday shelter. What will get you out and keep you out of trouble 99% of the times is something you always carry with you. It can never be taken away. You can take it when you travel. You will never be stopped by airport security nor will well-meaning legislators seeking to protect you from harm ban it. The most effective self-defense tool for detecting, avoiding, and confronting danger is the human brain and your willingness to follow some basic guidelines.

- **Don't Panic:** Panic is arguably your brain's greatest opponent when you are stressed or under attack.

Once panic takes control, you will become unable to protect yourself. Panic makes you think anything you do will be futile.

- **Stay in Control:** Fear will always defeat you if you allow it to take over. Fear can render you immobile and make you indecisive at the worst possible moment. It's okay to acknowledge fear, but you must be able to move and think in spite of it.

- **Be Flexible:** Your mind must remain flexible enough to accept what's happening. Once again, women have a distinct advantage as their thinking is not clouded or impacted by a sudden surge of testosterone, as are their male counterparts. Staying calm under pressure allows you to assess the reality of the situation.

- **Find Out What Is Going On:** Do a quick assessment and take action. Anything you do to get out of a situation is better than doing nothing.

- **Never Give Up:** Your brain is the engine that directs your body. It should never be the other way around. When confronting danger, never stop thinking about ways to save yourself. This powerful resource becomes even more formidable if you have taken the time to pack your experience library with a variety of well-thought-out action plans.

Personal Defense Resources

Whatever environment you find yourself in, there is always something that can be used to protect yourself. The following list is intended to jump-start your thinking process to recognize what "opportunities" surround you every day. Some items can be used to protect you from blows, while others will allow you to concentrate the full power of your blow into a single vulnerable target on an attackers body such as the a nose, temple, eyes, shins, or groin.

In an office

- A laptop computer can be used as a shield or striking tool.
- A stapler can be used as an impact weapon against an attacker's face or hands.
- Scissors or a ruler can be used for slashing.
- Power cords from phones can be used for whipping or binding.
- Anything on your desk that can be thrown can become a weapon.
- Pencils and pens can be used to penetrate an attackers skin.
- Any aerosol container can be sprayed in the eyes.

On an airplane

- A rolled up magazine can be used to attack the face or throat.
- A book can be used to block a blow or used to strike or be thrown.
- A blanket or clothing can be thrown over an attacker to disorient.
- Alcohol can be thrown into the eyes.

Your clothing

- Ladies high heels can be lethal if used like a hammer.
- Coats can be used as a defensive tool against sharp objects.

- Belts or a woman's purse can be swung.
- A sock can be filled with coins and used as an impact weapon.

At home

- A kitchen is a virtual arsenal with pots, pans, knives and more.
- Oven spray or bug spray.
- Flowerpots, stones from your driveway.
- Your workshop or garage offers opportunities ranging from hammers and screwdrivers to baseball bats and box cutters.

Always remember, if you find yourself in a situation where someone is trying to harm you, it is critically important to remain calm. As your mind clears, you will soon discover there are a multitude of items that can be used to protect yourself. If you can throw it, block with it, spray it, or crush with it ... you can use it to your advantage.

Keeping Safe During Disasters

FEMA, also known as the Federal Emergency Management Agency, suggests that you and every member of your family have what is called a "bug-out bag." For those of you not familiar with the term "bug-out bag" (also called a BOB, Get-Out-of-Dodge Bag, GO Bag, or 72-Hour Bag) it is an emergency backpack that has been equipped with items that will allow you to survive for up to three days. While many people plan their pack to sustain them for longer periods, there are limits to what you can carry.

What items you choose to put in that bag depends on how you intend to use it and where you are located. Your needs will differ depending on the time of year and whether you live in Alaska or Florida. Experts tell us there are several essential things that are necessary for survival. The most important is water. You can only survive three days without it. To that end, you should plan on each family member having two quarts a day for drinking. The primary purpose of a bug-out bag is to allow you to evacuate quickly should you be faced with a sudden disaster. If you don't want to pack a bag, at least take the precautionary step to gather all your materials and supplies in one convenient location.

The general recommendation is that a bug-out bag contains enough supplies to last each person seventy-two hours. Studies indicate it generally takes that long for disaster relief teams to arrive at an impacted area.

Must-have items typically include:

1. A copy of your passport, driver's license, plus an emergency contact list.
2. Multi-tool that includes items like pliers, knife, and saw blade.
3. A cell phone and means to charge it.
4. An 8'x10' tarp with 50 feet of nylon Paracord.
5. Candles, matches, and some type of fire starter.
6. Bottled water and protein bars.
7. First-aid kit and emergency blanket.
8. Feminine hygiene products.
9. Sun visor and water resistant windbreaker.
10. Cash in small bills.

11. Trash bag, hand sanitizer, and bleach wipes.
12. An emergency hand-crank radio.
13. Insect spray/repellent.
14. A mirror or some other type of signaling device.
15. A firearm with sufficient ammo (depending on location, legality, training)

CHAPTER EXERCISE

✓ What is your most powerful weapon in any situation?

✓ Why would water be the number one item in any GO Bag?

✓ Where would you go in the case of an emergency evacuation?

✓ How would you reunite with family members if you became separated?

✓ What items are in your immediate environment that could be used for self-defense?

"In the United States, a home burglary occurs every 13 seconds."

Federal Bureau of Investigation

8

Reacting To A Home Invasion

In 2012, one in four homes in the United States was targeted for a home invasion. Law enforcement authorities project home invasions will continue to rise because more traditional targets like gas stations and convenience stores are using security cameras and cash lockboxes. While most home invasions start off as a break-in or theft, they can quickly turn into a sexual assault if a woman is in the home. For this reason, all women need to know what to do in the case of a home invasion.

On July 23, 2007, Stephen Hayes and Joshua Komisarjevsky followed Jennifer Hawke Petit and her daughter Michaela Rose Petit home from a trip to a local grocery store in Cheshire, Connecticut. Several hours later Jennifer, along with her two daughters Michaela and Hayley Elizabeth Petit, would be killed during the course of a home invasion. The only survivor would be their father, Dr. William Petit, whom the criminals left bound and beaten in the basement of his home.

The tactics being used by home invaders today are becoming increasingly brutal with more than a third of all home invasions becoming physically violent. Having your home broken into is a frightening experience and undermines your sense of safety. Add into that equation intimidation, assault, and death threats and suddenly the crime of home invasion becomes an intolerable event for victims and survivors. While it is often said there is no correct response to a home invasion, there are things you can do that will help you survive the encounter.

As with most of the other techniques we discussed in this book, it is always better to contemplate how you are going to react to an event before it happens. Several years ago, my life was threatened by a disgruntled co-worker who, at the time, was anonymous. Because the threats came through the mail, not only were the police involved, but so were postal authorities and the FBI. Sending threats through the mail is a federal offense.

One of the first things the investigating agents suggested was that we establish a code word or phrase that everyone in the family could use in the event trouble occured. When selecting a code word or phrase, always select a sequence that sounds like normal conversation. If my wife called and asked me to cancel her or one of our children's appointments with Dr.Nelson, I would know she needed immediate help. In fact, any mention of the name Dr. Nelson in connection with any family member indicated that those specfic members were in trouble. We and our childern were instructed never to use the phrase unless it was a life or death situation.

We were also encouraged to provide the police with an interior sketch of our home that included where our children slept and critical features in the home such as stairwells and blind corners. The floor plan was designed to provide police with a usable roadmap upon entering. It was also suggested that we set up some type of safe room. At that time, our home had solid core doors so we made the decision to install deadbolt locks on each bedroom door. If a break-in occured, our children knew to lock those doors until we or the police came to their aid. We also practiced safety drills, similar to fire drills, so everyone knew how to escape from the home in case of an emergency. The 911 emergency alert system had not been developed at that time; however, we installed an alarm system that was connected to the police department and posted emergency phone numbers near all the phones.

Today, when equipping a safe room, the following items should be included: cell phone, flashlight, first-aid kit, food, water, and some type of defensive weapon such as pepper spray, a TASER, or a firearm.

As with any physical encounter, the greatest threat typically comes within the first few minutes. During a home invasion, a criminal's success depends on immediately instilling fear into the victims. Home invaders will often bring handcuffs, rope, and duct tape to bind all occupants. Initially it is best to pretend that you are weak and do not present a threat. Not being preceived as a defender will often diffuse the initial rage and allows the invaders to focus on their mission.

Invaders will use several types of psychological manipulation to increase intimidation levels. In addition to a show of force and display of weapons, one tactic is to separate family members into different rooms to create increased levels of uncertainty. They may also separate the women from the rest of the family in an effort to gain more control over the men by implying compliance will ensure the safety of women and female children. During initial stages, home invaders will demonstrate they are in complete control and can dominate any attempt to resist. While it might be particularly difficult for women to watch a loved one being physically assaulted, or taken off to another room, it is important that you stay in control of your emotions and begin to develop a plan. Your first priority should always be to have at least one family member escape in order to summon help. In the Petit case, it was the father who was able to escape and call for assistance. Invaders often feel less threatened by a woman and are less likely to watch you as closely, giving you more of an opportunity to escape.

When posssible try to establish some type of communication with your assailants. Rather than asking how your husband or son is doing, always use names to personlaize your family members. Try to buy as much time as you can as you go through the ordeal. You might offer to make them coffee or ask if they are hungry. While it may sound counterintuitive, reaching out and offering help makes you more human and increases the perception that you are not a threat. Never show weakness, cry, or appeal for mercy. Doing so can often produce the opposite reaction with some criminal types who find heartless pleasure in inflicting pain and emotional stress.

If your attackers attempt to put you in restraints with such items as rope or tape use one or more of the following methods that will help you get free.

- If you are being bound up, keep your arms and wrists stiff and slightly separated so that you will be able to wiggle your way out using the slack you have created.
- If you are going to be bound in duct tape, voluntarily put your hands out in front of you. Once again keep

your hands and arms slightly separated. When the opportunity presents itself, raise your hands above your head and then in a rapid downward bursting action, bring your arms down and open them across your chest and hips—breaking the tape.

▨ Any sharp object such as a broken piece of glass can be used to cut rope.

▨ You can create a friction saw using your shoe laces to burn your way through rope or plastic ties.

We are often asked if these techniques really work. The answer is yes. Not long ago one of our female instructors was doing a demonstration at a local police department. Officers were told to bind her feet and hands with duct tape and lock her in the trunk of a car. They were convinced she would be unable to escape. Within five minutes the trunk of a car popped open and our instructor walked away.

Once you have broken free from your restraints, it is to your advantage to get away from the situation as quickly as possible. There might not be another opportunity to escape. By this time, you may have also gathered some information about your attackers, their plans, and their projected timeline. If you are personally unable to escape, always keep trying to get at least one member of your household out of the home.

Our natural tendency is not to want to leave anyone behind; however, doing so may save the entire family. While some thought that Dr. Petit's leaving his family behind was distasteful, his actions were responsible for bringing the police to the scene. Even though his family did not survive the encounter, Dr. Petit was able to testify in court and saw his attackers sentenced to death for the crimes they had committed.

In addition to stalking, criminals will use a variety of methods to gain access to your home. While they may force their way in, the most comon approach is to simply walk in through an unlocked open door. Always be sure to keep all ground-level doors locked, including your garage door, which is the largest door in your house. Other techniques that are particularly effective against women is to gain access by pretending to make a delivery of flowers, or someone pretending to be a member of a religious order. Criminals have also been known to use small children selling cookies or other items as a way to gain entry. Small children have also been used to gain access through basement windows and pet doors that would be too small for an adult.

Another well-used ruse is to claim that they are doing work in the neighborhood and wish to give you a free estimate.They might say they were involved in some type of accident or state that there is a medical emergency and need to use a phone. Our advice is never open the door to a stranger. If you are a mother or grandmother with young children in your home who run to the door to open it, we suggest you install a peephole at their level. Once installed, tell them this is a new game of peekaboo and that they will be rewarded for identifying people before the door is opened.

Additional ways to add supplementary layers of protection to your home can include:

- Plant defensive shrubs such as rosebushes or other thorny plants under windows and in areas where someone could lie in wait.

- Put timers on several lights in your home. Also include one or more radios tuned to a talk radio or news station. Heard from the outside these sounds can replicate conversations occuring in the home.
- Install a wireless alarm system. Today these items can be found at Home Depot and Lowes. If your budget permits, hire a professional security company.
- Install motion dectors on all of your outside lights.
- Walk around your home at night and look in the windows to see what others can see when casing your home.
- Install curtains and remember to close inside doors to eliminate vision corridors that make it easy for somone on the outside to monitor your movement.

If you are curious about the outcome of the threat to my life, the solution was rather classic. The individual who sent the threatening letters held the note paper with his fingertips as he penned the message. The resulting fingerprints were then traced by the Federal Bureau of Investigation. Apparently this individual had once worked for a bank and as luck would have it, all banks at that time fingerprinted employees as part of the hiring process. Once his prints were identified, it was easy to connect him to the crime. Today, DNA retrieved from a stamp or envelope would have the same impact.

CHAPER QUESTIONS

✓ How do criminals gain acces to a home?

✓ Why is it important to appear weak when threatened?

✓ Why is it critical that someone escapes during a home invasion?

✓ Name five things you can do to your home to help stop an invasion.

"Roughly 38,000 carjackings occur in the United States each year ... 75% involve the use of a weapon as a way to intimidate the occupants to open the doors of the car."

Federal Bureau of Justice Statistics

9

Reacting To A Carjacking

The crime of carjacking has become so abundant that the Federal Government passed a law in 1992 making carjacking a federal offense. The law also prompted the FBI to form an investigative task force, which eventually discovered that the pattern of carjacking in the United States was not as random as one might believe. While both men and women can be the target of a carjacking women are often seen as easy targets and need to take extra precautions.

The report revealed that the individuals responsible for this type of crime profile potential victims who put themselves in a vulnerable position by stopping their car in these locations:

- At ATMs where thieves get both your car and money.
- In high crime areas.
- In residential driveways.
- At intersections with stop signs or lights.
- At gas stations where the thief gets a full tank of gas and your car.
- On freeway exits and ramps.
- In isolated areas such as parking lots, garages, or behind buildings.

Car hijackers are practiced in the art of distraction, and they prey on drivers who are unaware. Learning what strategies they use can help you avoid becoming a victim of this crime. The most typical carjacking is called "a walk-up" and occurs when you have just approached your car or when it is stopped at a light or stop sign.

- If you see a potential threat or suspicious activity, try not to stop.
- If you want to attract attention, lean on your car horn and don't stop until help arrives.
- Immediately lock all car doors the moment you get in.
- If a traffic light is red, slow down and give it time to turn green and then move quickly through the intersection.
- Driving in the far left lane will give you better odds if you need to make a quick U-turn to exit an area.
- If you are driving in an inside lane, leave space between you and the car in front of you. A quick rule of thumb is to always leave enough room so that you can easily see the rear tires of the car in front of you.
- Remember your car is a safe haven. It can also be your most powerful weapon. If threatened with a weapon, step on the accelerator, lean on the horn, and drive over the threat. Call 911 for immediate help.
- Always leave the car in gear if you are in questionable areas. Doors and windows should not be opened for anyone except law enforcement.
- Never allow yourself or passengers to be kidnapped, as the likelihood of survival is low if you are taken to a remote location. Take any and all action necessary to avoid capture. If necessary, crash your way between cars, jump the curb, drive down the sidewalk or run a

red light. In a life-threatening situation, you must do whatever is needed to put the odds of escape in your favor.

- If bumped from behind, or if someone abruptly stops in front of you to cause an accident, never get out of the car, lock all doors and put all windows up. Call 911 to report your location and details of the incident. At the same time, ask for a female police officer to come to your assistance.

- If you are followed, drive to a local police or fire station and ask for help. If those options are not available go to Home Depot, Lowe's or similar facility. Upon entering the store, immediately request assistance.

- A carjacker will often attempt to break a side window to gain entry. Not only will his actions startle you, he will also violently pull you out of the car. If such an attempt is in progress, stomp on the gas and exit the area.

Some police departments advise that you give up your keys and let the carjacker have your car. While that is one option, many things can happen to you and your passengers once you open the door. Complying with their request is no guarantee of safety. Your best defense is to prepare for an unexpected carjacking in advance.

CHAPTER EXERCISE

✓ *Why is it important for women to lock all doors upon entering a car?*

✓ *Is it safe to get out of your car if hit from behind?*

✓ *What should you do if you are followed?*

✓ *Why is your car a safe haven?*

"A Workplace Violence Survey published in 2012 found that compared to two years ago, over one-third of firms responding noted that incidents of workplace violence remained at approximately 45%."

Society For Human Resource Management

10

Preventing & Reacting To Workplace Violence

Ordinary citizens are encountering violence in their workplace so often that homicide is now listed as the second leading cause of death for women and men in the U.S. workplace. The majority of incidents tend to cluster in occupations that are attracting more women such as sales, real estate, marketing, health care, retail, and hospitality. Other areas of concern include enraged coworkers, angry relatives, revenge-seeking acquaintances, and customers who show up at job sites. What is unsettling is that workplace homicides committed by customers on employees are the fastest-growing type of homicide today.

These events are often heavily covered and dramatized by local and national media. As a result, they ultimately have a significant psychological and financial impact on employers, employees, and customers. Sensationalized reporting makes us feel unsafe in a place where we should be safe. Statistics show that over 60% of impacted employees will not return to work for several days following an incident of workplace violence. That statistic is in sharp contrast to almost 100% of employees who will return to work following other disasters such as hurricanes, fires, or flooding. Workplace violence exerts an expensive toll, with American businesses losing approximately $36-$40 billion a year. The costs include lost productivity, settlement costs, court appearances, and related legal fees.

Reporters covering these episodes typically describe incidents of workplace violence with a degree of shock. The reporter often asks how this otherwise "normal" person could have committed this type of crime. When the facts finally surface, we often discover that initial warning signs were ignored due to either political correctness or discounted by co-workers and management as just being silly ideas. The unwillingness to report issues is further compounded by colleagues who do not want to see an associate lose a job in the current economy. There is also an increased reluctance on the part of management and human resource departments who choose not to become involved because of potential legal repercussions.

While there can never be a definitive set of indicators to pinpoint someone who is at risk for committing an act of workplace violence, statistics indicate that **men are often the primary offenders**. The following list is a starting point and offers general guidelines to women and men on how to identify someone who might be a potential offender.

- A male between the ages of 35 and 50.
- Abuses alcohol and/or drugs.
- Doesn't accept responsibility.
- Blames others.
- Is severely depressed.
- Has a history of violence.
- Is romantically involved with an associate.
- Is obsessed with police work, the military, or weapons.

- Has worked for the company for a number of years.
- Has an odd personality and has difficulty getting along with others.

It wasn't that many years ago when the idea of going into a workplace and shooting your fellow employees was unthinkable. Today, incidents of violence are in the news on a regular basis. While the media focuses its attention on the tools that are used to commit these crimes, the true cause of workplace violence lies deep within an individual's mental state and the circumstances that surround their lives.

Like it or not we live in a society where the prospect of you or someone you know being the victim of a violent crime at work is a real possibility.

What are the typical sparks that can set people off in the workplace?

- Layoff.
- Bad evaluation.
- Failure to be promoted.
- Poor support and cooperation from management.
- Extreme stress.
- Being belittled.
- Poor communication.
- Mandatory overtime or reduced hours.
- Disparity of treatment.
- Last-minute rush orders.
- Major changes in work assignments with no clear direction.
- Work related misunderstandings.

As you read the above indicators, please avoid the temptation to point to one or more and draw the conclusion that a particular incident sparked the "unexpected" explosion. Typically, an investigation reveals that an individual's motivating stress levels had been building up over a long period of time.

To avoid the possibility of a potential workplace violence incident, employees must have a way to safely report their concerns without fear of retribution. At the same time, managers and supervisors must be willing to intercede and take an active part when issues are raised.

It is strongly suggested that companies establish workplace violence committees that include a mix of workers and managers who are able to interact on an equal basis. Women can and must play an important role on these committees. Insist that company management back away from a "Zero-Tolerance Policy" in favor of the establishment of a "Will-Not-Tolerate Policy," which provides far more flexibility to both employer and employees. Zero-tolerance policies, mostly favored in male dominated organizations, almost guarantee that even minor infractions of the rules would result in an automatic dismissal. Employees are more likely to report incidents or concerns if they know that the information they are providing will be used to help a coworker rather than having the employee fired. Knowing that someone will be dismissed for a minor infraction of company rules often results in "minor" incidents of sexual harassment not being reported.

Drilling down a bit further into the makeup of potentially violent individuals, we can begin to see that various personality types might be more susceptible to a buildup of tension. These types might include:

- **Player** – acts on impulse and generally displays exaggerated mood swings.
- **Stranger** – loses touch with reality and approaches the environment and work as though they are visiting rather than being engaged.
- **Runaway** – does everything in their power to avoid responsibility and take credit for work that was never done.
- **Narcissistic** – are only interested in their personal gratification and take little interest in coworkers, projects, or the good of the company.
- **Back stabber** – prefers to work behind the scenes undermining the credibility of management and coworkers or employees in an attempt to always make themselves look better.
- **Stoic** – never learns from their mistakes nor do they see the benefit of making changes that can help themselves or the organization. They will often repeat the same mistakes over and over again and see little connection between their actions and results.

The first thing to remember if you are in a position to intercede is "if you are out of control, you can not control the situation." With that realization in place, you can take the following steps:

- Maintain your cool.
- Speak in a lower tone of voice than your aggressor does.

- Never challenge the individual, use condescending speech, or act as a judge.
- Do not tell the individual to be quiet or to calm down.
- Listen and try to determine what might be upsetting him.
- Demonstrate empathy to gain control of the situation.
- Demonstrate respect for the individual and what he is saying without judging or reacting to what is being said to you.
- Paraphrase and play back what you just heard. Your conversation might go something like this. "Let me be sure that I understand what you're saying. You are telling me that you are upset because _____ happened and are looking for a way to solve the problem. Is that correct?"
- Engage the individual. Ask for a clarification as this approach puts you in a position of being seen as a supporter and someone to be trusted. You never want to be seen as someone who is sitting in judgment.

We are often asked how can someone determine if a co-worker is about to "go over the edge." The best answer is to rely on your woman's instinct or "gut feeling." It does not take long to get to know people's habits after you have worked with them for a while. If someone is suddenly becoming evasive, angry, or is making quiet threats, it is time to intervene. Exactly how to intervene will depend on the company and the company's policy for dealing with employees who demonstrate potentially dangerous behavior.

While the first step is to report your concerns to management, privately you should also begin to think how you would respond if you suddenly found yourself challenged in a hallway, parking lot, or other location by this individual.

Begin by thinking about your work environment and ask the following questions:

- Where are the nearest exits?
- Where do they lead?
- What is beyond the exit doors and where could you seek cover?
- Are you able to hide somewhere in the event of a disaster?
- Where could you barricade yourself if escape was not possible?
- How would you call for help or notify others of potential danger?
- What could be done if no help was available?
- Would you be safer if you always carried a fully charged cell phone?
- Do you have an electronic pass that can access restricted areas?

When terror occurs in the workplace, it is explosive and unexpected. While some people will run in blind fear with no plan, others will stand frozen in place, totally incapable of moving or making any type of decision. Some will panic and unknowingly run directly into danger. Others will simply scatter, not knowing what to do next. Why does this happen? The answer is more physical than intellectual.

A normal resting heart rate for an adult ranges from 60 to 100 beats a minute. A lower heart rate implies more efficient heart function and better cardiovascular fitness. A well-trained athlete, for example, might have a normal resting heart rate closer to 40 beats per minute (BPM). If your heart rate were increased to 115 BPM as a result of exercise, you would not experience any debilitating side effects. However, when fear drives your heart rate to the same level, you begin to lose fine motor skills such as the ability to unlock a door or dial a phone.

Fear creates an entirely different scenario because your system suddenly floods with adrenaline. Once your "fear factor" heart rate exceeds 145 BPM, it is almost impossible to execute many of the self-protection techniques that are taught in self-defense studios. At 175 BPM, you will experience tunnel vision, loss of hearing, time will appear to either speed up or slow down. You will also suffer from temporary long-term memory loss. It may take days or weeks before you can clearly recall the specific details of that event.

Under these circumstances, how can you regain a sense of balance? The answer is called relaxation breathing, and it is a technique that is used by surgeons, students, police, and anyone who may be facing a stressful event or encounter.

How To Perform Relaxation Breathing

Begin by thinking of your stomach (not your lungs) as a balloon that you are filling with air as you breathe in and emptying smoothly as you breathe out. To start, try the following exercise:

- Breathe in through your nose to the count of four.
- Hold your breath to the count of four.
- Breathe out through your mouth to the count of four.

- Hold your breath to the count of four.
- Repeat until you feel your body and mind relax.

You can vary this breathing count technique to fit your own needs. The overall goal is to create a smooth, continuous cycle of breathing. One bonus of this calming technique is that no one has to know you are doing it so it can be done inconspicuously in the middle of any distressing situation.

CHAPTER EXERCISE

✓ Name five potential identifiers of someone at risk.

✓ What three or four things might lead someone to violent behavior at your workplace?

✓ How can speaking in a lowered tone help control violent people?

✓ Why should women insist on a will-not-tolerate policy instead of a zero-tolerance policy at work?

✓ What happens when fear sends your heart rate to 145 BPM?

"When the Himalayan peasant meets the he-bear in his pride,

He shouts to scare the monster, who will often turn aside.

But the she-bear thus accosted rends the peasant tooth and nail.

For the female of the species is more deadly than the male."

Rudyard Kipling, The Female of the Species

11

What Every Woman Should Know

It is no secret that men and women think and behave differently. Men often view themselves as physically superior, simply because they possess greater upper-body strength. Women often presume that due to their smaller stature they cannot defend themselves against a male attacker.

Throughout history, women have led armies into combat, defended their homelands, and protected their families from uninvited guests. Jingu, for example, was married to the fourteenth emperor of Japan, Chuai, who reigned between 192 and 200 AD. After his death, she was quite comfortable leading his army to invade and conquer Korea.

Today, women from countries like the United States, Israel, Canada, New Zeland, Sweden, and many others can be found leading troops, flying attack aircraft, on board navel ships, and on the front lines of battlefields across the globe. When it comes to the preservation of personal safety, women also enjoy a strong presence in the ranks of police officers and firefighters around the world and compete with men on an equal basis.

In our **Girls Strike Back®** women's personal defense workshops, we begin each class by asking attendees if they would be comfortable defending themselves against a 6-foot, 250-pound male. Almost without exception, no one in the room will raise a hand—even those who have trained in martial arts.

We then ask the women to close their eyes and imagine the biggest, baddest, and ugliest attacker sitting in their backyard. When everyone is uncomfortable with the image they have conjured, we ask them what would happen if a squirrel jumped into the attacker's lap and he attempted to grab the squirrel with his bare hands. Almost everyone says the squirrel will win because it will bite and claw its way to freedom.

While the squirrel has the physical advantages of claws and teeth, few recognize that the animal possesses a far more powerful advantage. At no point during the confrontation does the squirrel give a second thought to how big the man might be, how he is dressed, or how intimidating his physical appearance is. All the squirrel knows is that something has grabbed on and that all hope for survival comes down to striking out immediately. The creature instinctively knows that he is in a fight for his life and automatically puts explosive energy into his response.

The next question we ask is, "If a small rodent weighing less than a pound can defeat a 250-pound male, wouldn't it seem reasonable that a woman weighing more than a pound might be able to achieve the same result?" At this point, most in attendance understand where we are going and that they are about to learn a self-defense method we call "fight like a squirrel."

While women tend to be nurturing, we often overlook that given the right circumstances and right training, everyone is capable of inflicting violence on another human being. Any woman can, if properly trained and motivated, defend herself against an attacker. While the methods and tools for self-defense may differ, we encourage each woman to have a plan in place that works for her. We asked them to consider what they would do if they were the victim of an attack. What would they do if they were being followed? What would they do if someone attacked their child, a favorite pet, or loved one? Would they choose to stand by and be a victim or would they choose to fight back to protect themselves and their family? When women are pressed to defend a loved one, the amount of determination to win is both impressive and potent.

The decision to defend life is a personal choice and only you can decide what is right for you. The fact that you might survive an assault does not necessarily mean you will go through the rest of your life unscathed. Survivors often suffer from long-term physical disabilities, experience flashbacks, and suffer from post-traumatic stress disorder. For some, the use of alcohol, drugs, or self-imposed isolation become lifetime coping solutions to escape past memories.

I have a personal acquaintance who was sexually assaulted over 30 years ago. Her voice still quivers whenever she speaks about the incident and confides that she did not resist her attacker out of fear of being hurt. Statistics show that when you resist an attack on your person, the chances of a positive outcome increase by as much as 70%. Win or lose you will always know in the back of your mind that you did everything in your power to defend yourself.

The majority of women who come to our workshops think of a sexual assault as a stranger jumping out of the bushes and attacking them. The good news is that this type of confrontation is the rarest and is the easiest to avoid. Simply by staying with a group of women, you decrease your chances by more than 90% of being singled out for an attack. Stranger rapes constitute the smallest percentage of sexual assaults and often occur in isolated areas. The overwhelming majority of assaults actually occur between people who know each other, sometimes superfically.

A personal assault is an unwelcomed form of human contact. Because two people are involved in this interface, you can exert a level of influence on future events. If you perceive that a person, place, or thing may present a threat to your personal safety, it is in your best interest to remove yourself from that situation. For example, if you decided to lie down on railroad tracks, you could reasonably expect that at some point you will be hit by an oncoming train. Simply said, if you choose to engage in high risk behavior, or associate with questionable people, life will eventually catch up with you. If you choose to walk across an empty parking lot at night because you are too embarassed to ask security to accompany you to your car, you are engaging in high risk behavior.

While there is no single profile to correctly identify a potential abuser or attacker, there are certain traits women can use as warning signs.

Some danger signs might include:

- The excessive use of alcohol and/or drugs.
- Habitually belittling others.

- Negative comments.
- Bullying.
- Excessive anger.
- Physical and vebal tantrums.
- Highly possessive or obsessive.

While there are other signs, those listed here are some of the stronger indicators. Not only can these be the warnings of a potential abuser, they can also indicate a propensity toward other types of anti-social or criminal behavior.

The best way to protect yourself is to use what we call a pyramid defense. Depending on the level of aggression you are facing, you can begin your self-defense protocol at any of the following levels and escalate or de-escalate your defense as appropriate.

- Base –   Walk away from any dangerous situation.
- Level I –   Have a plan in place **before** it is needed.
- Level II –   Consider how your personal habits can be easily patterned.
- Level III – Be aware of your surroundings.
- Level IV –   **Always** listen to and **trust** your intuition.
- Level V –   Establish eye contact; speak up loudly and clearly.
- Level VI –   Never go to a secondary location if threatened.
- Level VII – Learn to protect yourself using common every day items.
- Level VIII – Learn some form of self-defense.

Being female means that you have a one-in-four chance of being sexually assaulted during your lifetime. Age is no barrier.

Women can be assaulted as well into their 80s and 90s. You can choose to ignore the statistics or you can purchase "mental insurance" and develop senarios as to how you would react to a situation.

While women do not possess the same upper body strength as men do, a woman's legs are longer than a man's arms and they are potentially much stronger. Properly trainined women weighing under 125 pounds can successfully defend themselves against an attacker three times their physical size.

The best way to initially deter a predator is to distract him by engaging in an abstract discussion. Do not show emotion, appear frightened, or arrogant. Always strive to keep the tension low by using direct matter-of-fact phrases like:

- I am waiting for ... my husband, boyfriend, the police, etc.
- I am on duty (*whatever that means*) and it would be wise for you to leave right now.
- I am off duty (*on vacation*) right now but that can change if you continue.
- You need to stop what you are doing right now.
- Back off—said several times with increase volume.

The above phrases typically will result in someone backing off. You may recall in the introduction to this book I was approached by an armed attacker. My defense was, "Look, I just got off duty and I don't want to have to deal with anymore guys like you today. Get off this train before I change my mind." In that case the predator backed up and ran.

Sometimes a verbal offense will not deter a predator. Should the situation continue to escalate, do not hesitate to use pepper spray as a deterrent. This defense tool has no long lasting effects and is easily defendable in court in the event it was mistakely used against an "innocent admirer." Some of the most effective products on the maket today are made by SABRE. As a SABRE instructor I can verify that this product is extremely effective. It is the same product used by the N.Y.C. Police Department, the U.S. Border Patrol, and in many prisons across the country.

Another effective option is to pretend you are on your cell phone speaking with the police. As you conduct your conversation, point the cell phone at the individual and then ask the "imaginary officer" on the other end of the line if this is the individual they are looking for. Don't be bashful with this technique. A little bit of acting here goes a long way. One student told us a story about how she stopped unwanted advances by using her cell phone. She took his picture so the police could see he was not the person they were looking for. Sometimes the truth is stranger than fiction. All the time she kept walking away and carrying on her highly animated conversation with no one on the other end of the phone.

CHAPTER EXERCISE

✓ What are other ways women can defend themselves?

✓ Why are women often reluctant to ask mall security for assistance?

✓ Why is it important for women to stay with a group?

✓ What does fight like a squirrel mean?

"Domestic violence causes far more pain than the visible marks of bruises and scars. It is devastating to be abused by someone that you love and think loves you in return. It is estimated that approximately 3 million incidents of domestic violence are reported each year in the United States."

Senator Dianne Feinstein

12

Understanding And Preventing Intimate Partner Abuse

In the United States, a woman is beaten or abused by an intimate partner every nine seconds. While intimate partner abuse is preventable, it requires taking direct action.

After working with abused women for a number of years, we have come to the conclusion that it is much safer for women to stay away from a potentially dangerous relationship rather than trying to change an abusive partner or engage in a war of words or legal action. Consider the following:

Impacts On Adults

- Domestic violence is the leading cause of injury to women—more than car accidents, muggings, and rapes combined.
- Studies suggest that up to 10 million children witness some form of domestic violence annually.
- Nearly one in five teenage girls who have been in a relationship reported that a boyfriend threatened violence or self-harm if they broke up.

- Three or more women are murdered daily in the United States by husbands or boyfriends.
- Ninety-two percent of women surveyed list reducing domestic violence and sexual assault as their top concern.
- Domestic violence victims lose nearly eight million days of paid work per year in the U.S. alone; that is the equivalent of 32,000 full-time jobs.
- The cost of intimate partner violence in the U.S. alone exceeds $5.8 billion per year: $4.1 billion for direct medical and health care services, while productivity losses account for nearly $1.8 billion.
- Men who as children witnessed their parents' domestic violence are twice as likely to abuse their own wives than are sons of nonviolent parents.

Parents Are Not Aware

- 81% of parents surveyed either believe teen-dating violence is not an issue or admit they don't know if it is an issue.
- 75% of parents were unaware that their teen had been physically hurt or abused by their partner.
- 69% of parents were unaware that their teen was pressured by their partner to perform oral sex.
- 67% of parents were unaware their teenage daughter was "checked up on" by their boyfriend 30+ times per day.
- 54% of parents admit they have not spoken to their child about dating violence.

Intimate Partner Abuse Defined

Intimate partner abuse occurs between two people in any type of close relationship. The term "intimate partner" includes current or former spouses, spouses in the process of separating, and dating partners. Partner abuse also exists along a continuum from a single incident of abuse to ongoing battering. Abuse can be one way or mutual.

According to the Center for Disease Control, intimate partner violence is a serious, preventable public health problem that affects millions of Americans. The term "intimate partner violence" describes physical, sexual, or psychological harm by a current or former partner or spouse. This type of violence can occur among heterosexual or same-sex couples and does not require sexual intimacy.

The CDC notes four main types of intimate partner violence:

- **Physical violence** is the intentional use of physical force with the potential for causing death, disability, injury, or harm. Physical violence includes, but is not limited to, scratching, pushing, shoving, throwing, grabbing, biting, choking, shaking, slapping, punching, burning, use of a weapon, and use of restraints on one's body, or strength against another person.
- **Sexual violence** is divided into three categories:
  1) Use of physical force to compel a person to engage in a sexual act against his or her will, whether or not the act is completed.

2) Attempted or a completed sex act involving a person who is unable to understand the nature or condition of the act, unable to decline participation or to communicate unwillingness to engage in the sexual act because of illness, disability, the influence of alcohol or drugs, or because of intimidation or pressure.

3) Abusive sexual contact.

- **Threats of physical or sexual violence** occurs through the use of words, gestures, or weapons to communicate the intent to cause death, disability, injury, or physical harm.

- **Psychological/emotional violence** involves trauma to the victim caused by acts, threats of acts, or coercive tactics. Psychological/emotional abuse can include, but is not limited to, humiliating the victim, controlling what the victim can and cannot do, withholding information from the victim, deliberately doing something to make the victim feel embarrassed, isolating the victim from friends and family, and denying the victim access to money or other basic resources. It is considered psychological/emotional violence when there has been prior physical or sexual violence or any prior threat of physical or sexual violence.

- **Stalking** generally refers to harassing or threatening behavior that an individual engages in repeatedly, such as following a person, appearing at a person's home or place of business, making harassing phone calls, leaving objects or written messages, or vandalizing a person's property. Before beginning any discussion on how to walk away from an abusive relationship, it is important to recognize the fact that some women choose not to leave. The logical question that is often asked is "Why?"

A theory we support is that a battered woman experiences a powerful feeling of relief once an incident is over. If you were being pummeled or emotionally abused every day, wouldn't you be thankful when that abuse stopped? Over time, it is possible to become emotionally addicted to that feeling of relief and to the abuser who can deliver that peace. This phenomenon is quite similar to the Stockholm syndrome, which is the psychological tendency of a hostage to bond with, identify with, or sympathize with his or her captor. While outsiders see the abusive behavior as extraordinary, over time the victim takes it in stride. Victims who are constantly assaulted or ridiculed by an intimate partner often find themselves experiencing two conflicting emotions/desires:

- A strong desire to remain in a known environment.
- The natural instinct to flee when threatened.

While these conflicting desires defy all logic, no amount of reasoning appears to convince some abused women to leave a violent relationship. Police officers responding to domestic abuse incidents often find themselves being attacked by the very victim they came to help. Today, many states have enacted laws requiring that the identified abuser must be taken into custody because too often battered spouses refuse to press charges.

The key to escaping this emotional trap is for women to be aware of and recognize the early warning signs that they are going down a dangerous path. The longer you stay involved in the relationship, the more difficult it will be to leave. It is critically important in the early stages of any relationship that women stand up for themselves and their individual rights. If you find you are becoming the butt of jokes or the object of ridicule, it is your responsibility to challenge the abuser before his actions are repeated. You cannot ignore an abuser's behavior and hope that his behavior will change over time.

Women often believe, "If I'm nice to him, he will eventually be nice to me." The reality of the situation is that the nicer you are to any abuser or bully the more abusive they will become

In an attempt to seek comfort, women will often spend hours pouring out their emotions to close friends or family. While this effort has some therapeutic value, in the end, the only person who will be able to solve your problem will be you. Never expect an abuser to come to their senses and make amends. They will not. Sally Kempton said it well when she wrote "it's hard to fight an enemy who has an outpost in your head."

If your partner is emotionally bashing you on an ongoing basis, you can either:

- Choose to feel sorry for yourself.
- Talk with friends and family.
- Make a decision to get out and move on.

In addition to verbal, emotional, and physical abuse, abusers will take control of family funds, deny access to bank accounts, and shield their victims from all financial information. Abusers will also seek to control among other things a choice of clothing, selection of makeup, choice of friends, access to car keys, or the ability to make any type of purchases beyond an approved list of items. While these control measures are initially effective, over time the abused will begin to question the authority of the abuser. At this stage, any challenge to an abuser's authority will typically result in a swift and dramatic escalation of abuse.

Even though leaving is the best response, it is often at this point where most women are injured or killed. While women will often seek restraining orders, it is important to recognize that a restraining order will not stop a potentially violent individual.

If you believe you may be facing the threat of immediate physical danger or that you will become a stalking target after leaving a relationship, you will need to find ways to make yourself invisible or unavailable to the abuser. Finding and contacting a battered women's shelter may be your best solution. If you are planning on leaving a relationship, NEVER announce your intentions in advance and never use it as a threat in the hope that you will stop the abuse.

Work quietly to make your arrangements in advance so that you can exit the situation when your abuser is not watching. Having your credit cards, cash, and important papers ready to go at a moment's notice will give you greater flexibility and allow you to rebuild your life more quickly.

Once you leave, <u>never go back</u>. If you are dating someone or are involved at any level, when you decide to end that relationship never use tentative language such as, "I don't want to be in a relationship with you right now" or "We can still be friends." Such an approach suggests to your former partner and any of his intermediaries that you might be open to reconciliation at some future date.

When you leave, get caller ID on your phone and never answer his calls. If you answer your phone after X number of rings or calls, he will simply repeat the pattern time and time again. Never explain why you don't want a relationship; simply indicate that the relationship is over. Immediately stop all direct contact and cut off all contact with any friends or delegates who may try to approach you in an effort to achieve reconciliation.

Before getting involved in a relationship, women would be wise to check these early warning signs to see if your partner:

1. Uses symbolic violence like breaking or tearing things up.
2. Makes you intuitively feel you are at risk.
3. Breaks or strikes things in anger.
4. Uses alcohol or drugs as an excuse for bad behavior or violence.
5. Has a history of encounters with police on behavioral issues.
6. Is jealous of anyone who takes up your time.
7. Is verbally abusive.
8. Resolves most conflicts with intimidation or bullying.
9. Pushes you into making commitments early in your relationship.
10. Was abused as a child?
11. Blames others for problems of his own making.
12. Refuses to take responsibility for his actions.
13. Identifies with violent people in film or fiction or history.
14. Is inflexible and unwilling to change or compromise.
15. Engages in stalking.

16. Belittles you and makes fun of you in front of friends and strangers.
17. Projects extreme emotions that are out of proportion with reality.
18. Uses money to control your freedom.
19. Instills fear that you or your children will be hurt.
20. Uses male privilege as a justification for his conduct.
21. Uses weapons (guns, knives, etc.) as tools of intimidation

While more warning signs could be added to this list, your own instinct and intuition are probably the strongest indicators that you need to walk away. If any other signs trouble you, write them down so that you can accurately describe your concerns to others including law enforcement.

CHAPTER EXERCISE

✓ What is the first thing you should do if you are concerned about your partner?

✓ What are the three categories of sexual violence?

✓ Is it okay to remain friends after you break up with your partner?

✓ Is it true that if you are nice to your abuser, he will treat you better?

✓ Name five or more warning signs of a potential abuser.

"1 in 6 women and 1 in 19 men have been stalked during their lifetime. Two-thirds of the female victims of stalking (66.2%) reported stalking by a current or former intimate partner and nearly one-quarter (24.0%) reported stalking by an acquaintance."

National Intimate Partner and Sexual Violence Survey

13

Stopping A Stalker

If you are being stalked, you must take the initiative sooner rather than later and not be put into being the prey in a potentially deadly game of cat and mouse. It is critical to gain control by not playing the stalker's head game. Your best defense is to turn the tables by being proactive and becoming a predator to be feared.

- **Do not handle this yourself**. Call in anyone and everyone who can be of help, *and be specific in letting them know exactly how they can help.*
  Stalkers specialize in picking on people who *won't* call for help. Professional and independent women are often easy targets. Typically these women have a strong sense of self-reliance and are reluctant to ask for help for fear of showing weakness. Stalkers also specialize in targeting people who *just want the problem to go away* along with individuals who are at a loss as to what to do or say when accepted rules of behavior are violated.
- **Call your local women's crisis center**. Their hotline numbers can be found on line or in your local phone book. Various states and municipalities approach

the issue of stalking differently. A local center will be familiar with the specifics for your city or town.

The more you know, the less stress you will experience as you and the members of your support team work on the problem.

- **Give it time.** If you want this situation to go away, it will take time, work, and money on your part. If you have children and joint custody is involved, consider making arrangements to have your ex pick up your children at the local police station for his visits. This does several things:

  - First, it allows you to obtain a restraining order without violating his visitaton rights.
  - Second, it keeps you from having to deal with him.
  - Third, it gets everyone involved known by the police.

- **Consider getting a restraining order.** This is a critical step in establishing a paper trail. Your local crisis center will give you all the help you need in this regard. The value of a restraining order is not the physical protection it provides, rather it gives the police and the courts what they need to arrest and convict the stalker.

  A restraining order should not be taken lightly. Its purpose is to help you cut off any and all direct contact. Once it is issued, do not violate it by calling your ex or asking for help.

  If the stalking continues, you will need to provide evidence. Purchase a cell phone or digital camera that allows you to document any time the abuser is near.

  If the individual comes to your door at night, push the record button on the phone or camera and capture the incident. Keep a log of all harassing or hang-up phone calls.

- **Consider installing** an application on your cell phone like StopaStalker that allows you to collect information, collate it, and report it to authorities in a simple application specifically designed for victims of stalking.
- **On the Internet,** make sure your profiles are private and consider using different usernames for every form of social media you use. Avoid tagging photos or having your photos tagged as they can be tracked back to you.

  Do not respond to instant messages and do not threaten. If you intend to take legal action, don't announce it, just do it and do not back down once you have started.
- **If you find a note on your car,** do not pick it up and read it in public. Make a show of taking it from the windshield and crumpling it up and throwing it into the back seat of your car. If he is watching he will not get the satisfaction of seeing you react. Retrieve and save all notes when you are certain you cannot be observed. This type of hard evidence gathering is critical for enforcing a restraining order.
- **A final consideration** – Purchase some type of self-defense weapon since stalking can escalate into extreme violence. Consider purchasing law enforcement level pepper spray or a TASER, and attend a class on how to use it. Once you have heightened your situational and self-awareness levels, consider taking a self-defense class. You will be more prepared to fend off any type of attack and respond better physically than someone who is surprised by an

attack and must battle extreme fear and the adverse effects of adrenaline. You may not have control over what a stalker will do, but if you are physically attacked, you will have additional options at your disposal.

CHAPTER EXERCISE

✓ Why is it important for women to take control of the situation?

✓ Why does it take time for stalking issues to be resolved?

✓ How does involving more people help you stop a stalker?

✓ Why is pepper spray a good deterrent?

"The right to self-defense is a natural individual right that pre-exists the government. It cannot morally or constitutionally be taken away absent individual consent or due process."

Judge Andrew P. Napolitano

14

Understanding Violence

Both the American Psychiatric Association (APA) and the American Medical Association (AMA) have made unequivocal statements about the direct connection between media violence and violence in our society. While members of the media and other political support groups continue to deny the findings, the American Psychiatric Association 1982 report "Big World Small Screen" states that the facts are clear. The report notes that the scientific debate is over and reports that media violence directly translates to real violence. In 1992, the APA's Task Force on Television and Society published a second report that further confirmed the link between TV violence and aggression. Research suggests that portrayals of violence against women in the media can increase the acceptance of sexual violence and rape myths such as "she was asking for it" or that women regularly make false claims of rape.

Today violence is not just an American problem; it has become and international issue. Assault rates are skyrocketing worldwide as the media and entertainment industries continue to promote violence as a way to increase sales and gain greater market share. News editors across the world support the doctrine of "if it bleeds it leads" when it comes to leading news stories in newspapers, magazines, and on our airwaves.

The net result of this never-ending bombardment of violence by the media and video game industry has conditioned us to accept increasing levels of violence as normal. Consider the following:

- By the time an average child finishes elementary school, he or she will have seen an average of 8,000 murders on TV.
- By the age of 18, he or she will have seen over 200,000 violent acts.
- 79% of Americans believe TV violence helps precipitate real life chaos.

Our Canadian neighbor has always been considered to be relatively crime free and stable. As a nation they have strict gun laws, a paternalistic government, and a strong sense of community. Yet inspite of their laws, the number of assaults and violent crimes are now increasing at the same rate as violent crime in the United States. The finding strongly suggests that media violence, not access to weapons, is a breeding ground that encourages real violence in every society.

Just as the earth's magnetic field protects us from the sun's harmful rays, culture and strong family traditions can act as a protective bubble to isolate its members from the constant barrage of media violence. Japan is an outstanding example of how family ties and respect for others has successfully contained the impact of media violence over their many generations.

While both the U.S. and Japan show equal amounts of violence in their respective media, research has shown that compared to American shows, Japanese programs also emphasize the consequences of violence. The modern-day hero in Japanese drama, much like the classic samurai figure, is noble, honest, highly disciplined, and hard working. When these heroes are wounded or killed, it arouses distress and evokes sympathy rather than applause as seen in other nations.

Once a segment of society is predisposed to violence, suggestions by the media can serve to enflame those who are caught in a never-ending cycle of poverty, drugs, gangs, discrimination, and the availability of illegal firearms. Over time, the constant drum beat of media violence dulls the senses and creates an environment where using verbal and physical violence to solve social or economic issues is accepted.

I recently had an opportunity to speak with a young man who was shot while on the streets of Hartford, Connecticut. He was shocked to discover that the wounds he received were actually quite painful. He had seen people shot on television and knew from his "media experiences" that people were able to carry on conversations without pain or discomfort. So much for truthfull depictions of reality on the small and big screens.

If you are reading this book, chances are good that you routinely conduct yourself in a civilized manner. We can presume that you interact with others in a respectful way. You probably have been successful in your career because of the way you interact with other people. The topic of violence may make you feel uneasy or be repulsive or offensive to discuss.

As human beings we have a natural built-in resistance toward injuring another human being. On the other hand, as a society we are as fascinated by killing as we are by sex. Ask any soldier returning from combat what question he is most often asked. You'll soon discover the number one question is "How many people have you killed?" In a similar fashion, police officers routinely report that children as young as five years of age will ask if they have ever used their firearm to shoot someone.

Those who have experienced true violence will often ignore the question or answer it in general of terms. In contrast, those who brag about how they used violence are typically trying to impress someone. Thankfully, true violence is something we do not encounter often but when we do, you must know how to react. The most likely reponses include:

- **Fleeing.** The first response to any type of danger should be to step back, evaluate the situation, and leave the area.
- **Posturing.** Here we initiate a combination of physical and verbal indicators that hopefully will stop further escelation. Males will typically stand taller or assume a strong stance in an effort to say "back off." Ideally these actions will send an intimidating message— without the need to engage in actual physical contact.
- **Fighting.** This should not be viewed as a casual exchange of punches. In a life-and-death situation, your intention should be to deliver significant damage to your attacker by any means possible. If you can talk your way out of and escalating situation, that should be your first choice. It is not a sign of weakness. However, if you are seeing that diplomacy is not working, wait for an opportunity to attack. Once you make this

decision, do not stop until your attacker is unable to continue his assault.

- **Submitting.** Here you acknowledge that your attacker has superior skills and signal that there is no need to continue the conflict. Unfortunately, submission may not always be the best option. For some aggressors, sensing weakness will immediately escalate their attack. Surviving an encounter may mean that you will suffer a combination of lifetime injuries or psychological damage.

Options at your disposal might include the following:

- Use of pepper spray.
- A strike to the groin.
- A thumb into an eye.
- A strike to the throat.
- Breaking a finger.
- Biting or choking.
- Using a force multiplier (a cane, pen, umbrella, car keys, in short, anything that will allow you to inflict damage.)
- Armed self-defense (knife, firearm or weapon of opportunity.)

You don't want to get into a violent encounter. If you are faced with a situation where you have no choice, you will have to decide what type of action you'll take. There is no right or wrong answer, it is up to you as an individual to decide in advance how you will handle a life treatening situation.

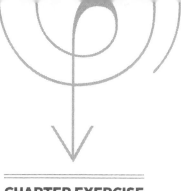

CHAPTER EXERCISE

✓ *What does the APA say about violence in the media?*

✓ *What options do you have when facing danger?*

✓ *Is talking your way out of a fight or walking away a sign of weakness?*

✓ *What influence can you have on the media to stop promoting violence?*

✓ *Ask yourself under what circumstances you could you injure someone to protect yourself?*

"Give a person a fish and you will feed them for a day; teach them to use the Internet and they won't bother you for weeks."

Unknown

15

Personal Safety On The Internet

Some of the greatest events that have impacted the course of human history include the invention of the wheel, the Industrial Revolution, the Guttenberg printing press, and modern medicine. Today we are participating in an equally significant event —the emergence of the Internet and the convergence of multiple technologies that allow us to connect with the world with the touch of a button.The implications of this new technology is changing the way humans have communicated since the beginning of time. Interconnectivity is impacting every aspect of our personal lives including our privacy and personal safety.

According to the Pew Research Center, women are significantly more inclined to use social networking sites than men in nine out of ten surveys they conducted. The findings suggest that women, due to their considerable presence on various social sites, need to exercise extreme caution. For these reasons we included the observations of Patrick Gray, former FBI Agent who investigated computer crime and intellectual property theft for the bureau.

Guest Contributor – Patrick Gray

As a twenty year veteran of the Federal Bureau of Investigation (FBI), I have seen the best and the worst of people when dealing with them in person and on the Internet. It is one thing to try to recognize those situations where you may feel discomfort because of your surroundings, and another thing to utilize situational awareness when cruising the Internet.

We know a seedy area when we see one in the physical world or recognize that a sparsely populated area or lonely subway station might not be the right place to be. On the Internet, the gloves are off. As an IT professional who has spent many years chasing down miscreants or working with businesses, schools, universities, and government agencies to strengthen their online presence, I can see how easy it is for people to let their guards down almost on a daily basis.

Two things have intensified this situation:

- Social Networking
- Mobile Devices

Social Networking

Large segments of our population are joining Facebook, Twitter, LinkedIn, Pinterest, Google+, YouTube, FourSquare, and other social networks. We are joining the fray because, well, we're all social animals. These sites are establishing relationships via our own personal networks or via friends of friends of friends.

The rub is that we don't know what we don't know. Most users are genuine, but because it is so easy to hide your real identity, it is possible to come into contact with people you would normally avoid. Once, the only way to invite friends and acquaintances to a party by phone or by hand-delivered or mailed invitations. Today, a young person can let their friends know about their birthday party by posting the information about when and where on their social networking site. Within seconds, hundreds of people potentially end up knowing about the party and often many turn up uninvited. The party can eventually turn into chaos with people getting angry and even refusing to leave. Often the police must be called in to turn people away.

By the same token, we are so enraptured by what we are seeing on these social sites that we want to join the fray. I know people who check in on Facebook wherever they are—local gas station, store, burger joint, park, or anywhere else, leaving a real time digital trail. Again, a person with criminal intent knows where you live—because it's on your profile; knows your date of birth—because it's on your profile; knows just where you are—because you just checked in; knows now that there's no one at home and recalls that you just purchased a new HD TV and an iPad, all because you told everyone in the world!

Pictures and videos can be shared easily across the Internet, so make sure you are careful when uploading—even if you only share it with friends, it can easily be spread much further than that.

Wise up! No date of birth other than the month and the day. No addresses of where you live—your friends will know because you have invited them over before and no checking in!

Tell people that you went to Hawaii after you get home, not while you're away!

You might say, "But Patrick, it's so much fun to be out there!" I know, but unfortunately there are bad apples everywhere who could care less about your online happiness.

Mobil Devices

The small device you carry on your hip or in your purse or backback has the ability to reach millions of people across the world with the touch of a send button. Never underestimate its power.

We see many instances of online stalking taking place because of the amount of personal information we reveal each and every day! Remember, you can be anyone you care to be. Do your remember the saga of Carlos Danger? Carlos is an excellent example of an online pseudonym that was used by former congressman and wannabe New York City Mayor Anthony Weiner during his online sexual chats with women. His use of the Internet destroyed his reputation and negatively impacted his career.

Women and girls are the usual targets of an ex-boyfriend or spouse who has a bone to pick or perhaps when a relationship turns sour. Or it can be a random foray based upon the type of information, including pictures that we display for all to see.

Inappropriate content? What better place than the Internet? You can find "anything " on the Internet. Pornography, personal abuse, and horrific crimes are In real time, we are vulnerable to pornography, personal abuse, and horrific crimes. One of the most heinous threats are pedophiles. We call inappropriate contact from pedophiles, grooming. At the FBI, we had many, what we labeled, Innocent Images Task Forces that targeted these predators who engage in inappropriate behavior toward a young person, putting them at risk to a sexual offense. The Internet makes it much easier for pedophiles to groom their victims. Monitoring your children's activity on the Internet is a must. Tell your daughters and sons never meet anyone they just met on the Internet at a physical location.

Every day we hear of instances of identity theft. The more information you make available online, the greater your risk of identity theft. As I have mentioned, It can be very tempting to post information about yourself on social networking sites, but you should never do it. Don't give out any addresses. Your close, personal friends will already have that information. Lastly, don't share any information about your banking on these social sites. While this may seem like common sense, we have moments of our own personal senility when we forget. Don't do it.

I've always been a stickler for robust passwords. Unfortunately, most of us use the same password for every account we have on the Internet. A robust password contains a mix of letters, numbers, and special characters. You may know that, but how many actually adhere to it? Create a sentence about something you know, are, or did. For example, "I graduated from Centennial High School in May, 1980." So, here's your password: IgfCHS5/80. Or, "My dog Peanut is 6 years old!" MdPi6yo! Robust and easy. You can actually write these passowords down as a sentence, stuff them in your wallet or purse and no one will have a clue as to what they are or what they mean.

We love to download stuff. Be it games, applications, coupons, or whatever, always read the fine print before hitting "download," More often than not, there is some sort of shareware attached such as anti-virus, other games, etc. Look for that small box at the bottom of the page that, if left unchecked, means that you tacitly agree to have the company share your personal information with other vendors.

Beware of spoofed emails that claim to be from the IRS, eBay, Craigslist, or even the FBI, claiming that they need information from you to update their files. Do not reply and please forward the email to the company or agency that it purports to be from. Because, if it is a spam message or a virus, you'll be infected and can suffer losses.

It's is a brave new word out there—beware of what your do not understand.

CHAPTER EXERCISE

✓ *What unique password system can work for you?*

✓ *How secure are your personal profiles on various social media sites?*

✓ *Name five confidential items that would be wise to remove from your social site(s)*

"We live in a wonderful world that is full of beauty, charm and adventure. There is no end to the adventures we can have if only we seek them with our eyes open."

Jawaharlal Nehru

16

Travel Safety

In addition to being a speaker and self-defense instructor, Jennifer Lownik, co-author of this book, is a professional meeting planner who has traveled domestically and internationally for the past 15 years. This chapter points out the many lessons she learned on how women can travel safely.

Women often face greater obstacles than men do, especially when traveling alone. However, a bit of careful planning, common sense, and respect for religious and societal differences, will allow you to minimize your risks and maximize your chances of having a safe and successful trip.

Know The Risks

The more you know about where you are going, the safer and better off you will be. When traveling abroad, sign up for the Smart Traveler Enrollment Program (STEP). Enter information about your trip so the Department of State can assist you in an emergency. U.S. Department of State Travel Warnings are a source for country-specific travel safety information.

Visit their site at http://travel.state.gov/travel/travel_1744. html.

- Take photos of your credit cards, I.D. cards, frequent flyer cards, prescriptions. (E-mail these to yourself along with the first and last numbers in your travelers check series.)
- Contact your cell phone company on how to get connected abroad **before** you leave home.
- Cover your passport to conceal American identity.
- Guard your passport. In some countries it can be worth $25,000 on the black market.
- Avoid clothing that identifies you as an American (ex: athletic wear for sports teams, colleges, etc.).
- Build a drop wallet (a throw away wallet for thieves).
- Avoid expensive accessories (jewelry, sunglasses, luggage).
- Try not to ask for help with luggage as it makes you look weak.
- Find out which areas to avoid before leaving. Confirm with hotel staff upon arrival.
- Never post travel plans on social media or discuss in public places.
- Tell people about your trip when you return, not while you are away.
- In your home, install timers on a television, lights, and a radio.
- Mount motion detector lights on the outside of your home.
- Have someone pick up mail, papers, flyers, mow the lawn, clear snow, etc. Be sure to turn off water to household appliances.
- Forward your home phone to your cell or another trusted phone.

Overseas Driver's License

It is illegal to drive without a valid license and insurance in many countries. You should check with the embassy of the country where you plan to drive and find out more about license requirements.

Driving To Your Local Airport

- Drive yourself or get a ride from someone you know and trust.
- Park in attended lots.
- Always give a vague return time to parking attendants when checking in.
- Never leave house keys with car keys and remove all personal information from car.
- Note the mileage on you car when checking in. Lock or remove GPS equipment.

Airport Safety/Destination Airport Safety

- Areas around airports and ground transportation are high-risk locations. Minimize time spent in these areas. Avoid staying at airport hotels.
- Schedule direct flights if possible.
- Avoid dress and behavior that may draw attention.
- Watch for people observing your schedule.
- Make a mental note of safe havens, i.e. police stations, hotels, or hospitals.
- Develop a plan(s) in advance for dealing with emergencies.

- Keep a close eye on your belongings, and do not get distracted.
- When going through airport security, pace your body with your belongings.
- Your life may depend on how fast you can exit a plane in an emergency. Always avoid high heals and tight skirts when traveling.
- When flying, count the number of seat backs from your seat to the nearest emergency exit.

Always Travel Light

You are much less of a target and more independent when you are not weighed down with a lot of luggage.

- The ideal handbag or daypack is easy to carry, has zippered inner compartments for added security,and a sturdy shoulder strap or harnesses. Carry your bag in front of you, close to your body, where it is out of reach of wandering hands. Carry only items that are lightweight and that you can afford to lose.
- **Always have at least one hand free at all times**. Consider wearing cargo pants or a vest with multiple pockets to store travel documents and gear.
- Use a money belt to conceal important items such as your passport, airline and train tickets, credit and debit cards, traveler's checks, cash, and medical prescriptions.
- Keep copies of all important travel documents in your suitcase in case the originals are stolen or lost.
- Use a small wheeled suitcase or backpack for long trips, a small day pack or tote bag for shorter

excursions. Keep luggage locked at all times and carry two sets of keys.

- Use luggage tags that hide your contact information from the inquiring eyes of thieves and con artists.
- Never carry anything across a border for someone.

Crime-Proof Yourself

Here are some easy ways to stay out of trouble:

- Be careful who you trust. Watch out for criminals—both male and female—who target women travelers. They may work individually or in teams, often posing as good Samaritans or creating distractions to steal belongings.
- Lower your tourist profile and try not to give the impression that you are lost or vulnerable. Know where you are going, what you are doing, and how to get back. Always carry the address or a business card from your accommodations. Avoid opening a map in a public area or keep it hidden under a newspaper. If you get lost, ask for directions from a police officer, shopkeeper, or find a phone and call your hotel.
- Use only legal and reputable taxis. Never hire a taxi if the driver approaches you in an airport arrival area. Such services are usually illegal and may be unsafe. Ask your hotel to recommend taxi services and avoid the risk of hailing an unlicensed cab on the street. Remember to take advantage of women-only taxis in such cities as London, Cairo, and Moscow. Driven by women drivers and only available to women passengers, these offer women an added level of

personal safety. Whenever possible, pair up with someone you trust when traveling by taxi. Male drivers have been known to take advantage of women who are traveling alone.

- Do not be afraid to make a scene. A loud whistle or even a healthy scream can be helpful tools to ward off an attacker, deter an intruder, or summon aid.

If Going Solo

When traveling on your own, be sure to follow these safety measures:

- Steer clear of isolated situations that could put you at risk. On a bus or train, sit next to someone of your own sex. In a taxi, sit in the back behind the driver. Avoid traveling in train carriages where you are the only passenger.
- Never go walking, jogging, or sightseeing alone in secluded areas, especially at night.
- If touring solo for the day, leave a note in your room explaining where you are going. If you do not return as planned, this information could be used to track you down.
- Take extra precautions if you go out at night. Understand that, in many parts of the world, "decent" women do not go out alone after dark, and doing so could put you at risk. Consider joining a sightseeing tour if you want to experience the sights and rhythms of a foreign city at night.

Finding Safe Accommodations

- Travel early in the day so you will have time to find a suitable place before dark. Book your lodgings in advance, especially if you are due to arrive late at night.
- Make sure you are comfortable with your accommodations and its location. Always ask to see the room before taking it. Does the door lock properly? Are there holes in the door or walls that could be used by peeping Toms? Are there fire alarms and escape routes? Does it feel safe? Do not stay anywhere unless you feel comfortable. Trust your instincts. If it does not feel right, make a change.
- You should always be vigilant. Ensure the door of your room is locked, even when you are inside. If someone claims to be a staff member, verify with the front desk if the person is authorized to enter your room.

Strictly Business

In many parts of the world, the concept of a career woman is highly unusual.

- **Get** thoroughly acquainted with your destination country's customs and business protocol, especially in cultures where women do not generally hold key corporate positions.
- **Always** meet your business contacts in the lobby of your hotel. Avoid giving out your room number. In some societies, it is forbidden for a woman to touch

a man in public. When in doubt, wait for the man to
initiate handshaking.

- **Dress** appropriately. If local women do not wear
slacks to the office, neither should you. Wear shoes
that allow you to stand for long periods and to move
quickly.
- **Be aware** that, in some cultures, even though you
do business with men in the daytime, women may
be required to sit separately for the evening meal.
Men may also steer clear of you in countries where
unrelated persons of the opposite sex aren't normally
left alone together.
- **Understand** that businessmen in certain societies may
think it is okay to flirt with or proposition you. A firm
"no" is appropriate.

What To Wear At Your Destination

Dressing for success varies from culture to culture. Defying
these customs may in some societies put you at risk.

- Find out what women wear in your host country
before you arrive. Pack a suitable wardrobe based on
your research.
- Err on the side of modesty—or dress conservatively—
if you want to blend in. The dress code is especially
strict in some male-dominated societies where bare
shoulders, short pants, mini skirts, and other revealing
attire may cause offence. A shawl can be a priceless
part of your wardrobe.
- Be prepared to cover your entire body, with the
possible exception of your hands and face in certain

Middle Eastern countries. Bring loose, linen trousers, a long-sleeved tunic, plus any mandatory head covering, Pack both sandals and shoes in case your feet must be covered.

Hotel Safety

- Carry a flashlight and bring a rubber wedge to put under inward opening doors.
- Request rooms above street level as street-level rooms provide easy access for intruders
- Request rooms below the fifth floor for ease of emergency evacuation.
- If you must let someone into your room, keep the door open and do not follow them in (room service, maintenance, housekeeping).
- Hang a "do not disturb" sign on your door when you leave and always leave the TV or radio on.
- Count the number of doors between your room and the fire stairs so you can find the exit in an emergency.
- Check in as Mr. and Mrs. if you are a solo woman traveler. Do the same if ordering room service.
- Do not leave valuables in your room. If you must travel with valuables, secure them in the hotel safe at the front desk. (In-room safes are not safe!)

Arrests Abroad

- If arrested, immediately ask to speak to a consular officer at the nearest U.S. Embassy or Consulate.
- General assistance – http://www.oncallinternational. com/enroll

CHAPTER EXERCISE

✓ What five "must-have items" can help keep you safe while traveling?

✓ Why is it not safe for women to hire any cab at an airport?

✓ When traveling solo, what is the best way to let others know where you are?

✓ How can you lower your tourist profile?

A Final Thought

In 2005, David Foster Wallace, an award-winning novelist and then professor at Pomona University, presented a commencement address to the graduating class at Kenyon College. He told the story of two young fish who, while swimming, pass an older fish going the other way. As the old codger passes he nods and says, "Good morning boys, how's the water?"

The young fish nod back and after swimming a little further on, one turns to the other and says, **"What the hell is water?"**

While David's story brings a few laughs, his message is clear—most of the time we chose to ignore the obvious realities of life, which in turn, are the hardest to see or talk about. By choosing to ignore the real world around us, we often put ourselves at great risk.

Hopefully this book has given you some time to think about the many changing environments you "swim in" each day.

Being prepared with a plan before you need one and knowing how to disengage and deflect conflict are the best ways to avoid struggles as you journey through the sea of life.

Be safe and be aware.

Epilogue

The story of women's safety is a long serious discussion that continues to be developed as women move further and further into the business world, into various cultures, and even into newer styles of relationships. As women, we are learning to move into situations we have not confronted in the past and it requires that we recognize the need to know beforehand what we need to do to keep ourselves safe and without being fear-filled. Life is meant to be enjoyed and lived with passion, smartly and yet with a willingness to expose ourselves to new situations and new dreams.

"What To Know Do And Say To Be Safe" is a book that was long overdue. It provides women with the necessary tools for addressing safety in every area of our lives, work, play, and life itself.

Sadly, in our personal lives, often the most dangerous of these areas, is where we most need to focus on being safe. Due to either our professional success or because of the increased expectations we bring into our relationships, women are asking for a newer style of relationship, a newer role in relationships with equal say in how the relationships develop or how they are simply lived.

For some men this new reality can become disheartening, and for someone who otherwise would never have resorted to violence but who is not used to being challenged, frustration and rage can come into play. In other circumstances it may be simply that a man has grown up with violence in his own home and it has become a learned reaction for dealing with anger or rage. If this is your situation, accept that it is not your job or your responsibility to love him out of his patterns. Doing so is a recipe for disaster. Only he can change his behavior and only if and when he wants to. As is so often pointed out in this woman's guide to personal safety, **nothing you can do or say will impact his behavior and certainly not before additional abuse takes place.**

When it comes to the specific topic of intimate partner abuse, research clearly shows that women most often are, or were, in an intimate relationship with their abuser prior to any incident of abuse. The greatest weakness women experience is denial because it keeps women vulnerable. "This is a onetime thing," "He didn't mean it," "He's not the type" are all reactions to situations which really cause you to discount what you know intuitively. Simply put, to deny what you know is truth.

When you continuously give up what you sense in your body, in your gut, what you know is real, because you don't like what it has to say, you come to rely on the others in your life and what they want you to believe. That is giving your power away and eliminating the built-in strength you have for staying safe. Know yourself, acknowledge what you know and always trust your instincts.

When you learn to trust yourself, you will begin to feel an inner power and confidence. This newfound strength prevents you from becoming so emotional that you lose your control. Consequently learning to trust yourself allows you to stay logical and intuitive, hear what isn't said, see what isn't obvious, and know what can't be easily explained. Although there are never any guarantees, whether dealing with a potentially abusive co-worker, lover, spouse, family member, stalker, or stranger, knowing your real strengths is of utmost importance.

Men's perceived strength may come from their physical size or aggressive approach. However, for women, that strength is in their ability to be assertive, never intimidating, which is a strength that doesn't cause another to feel threatened. Combined with instinct, it provides you with the ability to stand your ground, state your intent, and allow others to save face while making certain you are quietly taking control of the situation while keeping yourself safe.

Know your environment, know the laws, and most importantly, know yourself. Stay safe, stay assertively powerful, and intuitively connected. This is your life and your journey. Enjoy it, safely!

Dorothy A, Martin-Neville, PhD

Ordering Extra Copies Of This Book*

Individual copies of this book can be purchased by visiting http://www.amazon.com.

Consider Applying For Grants Or For Instructor Certification

Organizations are urged to contact the IM-SAFE Institute to apply for training to underwrite the costs for on-site women's personal safety programs.Alternatively, individuals can be certified as IM-SAFE instructors and be authorized to run in-house programs for your organization. Call 860-651-9611 for additional details.

*NOTE: A portion of the sales from this book will be donated to the IM-SAFE Institute, a 501(c)3 corporation to provide free training for women who have been impacted directly or indirectly by abuse. Contact IM-Safe directly for information on bulk book orders.

About The Authors

DENNIS E. GOLDEN, MA is the CEO of IM-SAFE® LLC, an organization dedicated to conflict resolution and personal safety education/training. A certified personal security professional, Dennis travels nationally and internationally. Thousands have attended his programs. A professional member of the National Speaker's Association and past president of the National Speakers Association Connecticut, Dennis also serves as an advisor and board member for several other organizations.

JENNIFER LOWNIK is a certified self-defense instructor and personal security specialist. She joined IM-SAFE® as Executive Vice President in 2006. Her inspiration came from personal life-changing events that she now shares with her audiences nationwide. Having spent more than a decade working with women and victims of assault, it was clear that women often did not take the time away from their careers or family to learn life-saving skills. She knew a new approach was needed.

Jennifer also serves as President of the IM-SAFE Institute a 501(c)3 non-profit corporation that provides conflict resolution training to women who have been impacted directly or indirectly by abuse at home or in the workplace.

Need A Speaker?

Dennis Golden and Jennifer Lownik are highly sought-after professional speakers whose expertise and focus is on personal safety, travel safety, and women's personal safety.. Featured on Fox News and other media outlets, Dennis and Jennifer are often the keynote presenters for national associations, corporations, and non-profit organizations across the U.S. and Canada.
For more information contact us at:
www.im-safe.com

Most Demanded Topics

Dangers of Traveling Solo
Preventing & Reacting To Workplace Violence
Engaging By Disengaging ~ Conflict Resolution
It's Not **What** You Said It's **How** You Said It
What Women Don't Know About Personal Safety
Inside The Mind Of A Predator
Resolving Conflict At Work, At Play, In Life

Made in the USA
Lexington, KY
10 August 2014